To Lyle —

God Bless!

Eph 2:10

"Whereas the majority of training concepts deal with surface issues and behavioral problems exhibited by people at work, the 'Molitor Process' addresses core dilemmas, attitudes, and values that when resolved have a life-changing effect on the lives of individuals, both at work and beyond."

—Kamal Bengougam, publisher, ETHOS *(Ethics in Business) magazine (United Kingdom)*

"Brian D. Molitor speaks with authority based on years of experience, and he backs up what he says with true life examples of how to do it right—and wrong. He captures the essence of management's struggle—truly implementing change—and makes it palatable, possible, and manageable. Molitor's balanced approach isn't full of management philosophies that sound great but never change the bottom line. He speaks as one who has been in the trenches and is willing to take you with him to the other side. He has taken his own words to heart and is changing his world. *The Power of Agreement* is a must-read for every manager or manager-to be."

—Guy Carlson, publisher, Christian Businessman *magazine*

"*The Power of Agreement* is a blend of simple but powerful concepts (i.e., followership development) supported by real-life experiences that are key elements in managing change. I strongly recommend this book to anyone looking to lead an organization toward teamwork and teams. Brian's insight on personal relationships and cultural change is the catalyst that makes the Molitor development process work!"

—Fred Dailey, plant manager, Witco Corporation (West Virginia)

"In *The Power of Agreement,* Molitor clearly shows the importance of quality leadership and the need for agreement—agreement on goals, core values, and corporate strategies. There is something in this book for everyone, employer and employee alike. The truths in this book are usually simple ones, but they are often neglected much to the detriment of the modern corporation in America. Molitor provides helpful examples and case studies from his own work as a troubleshooter and consultant."

—Dr. Burton Folsom, senior fellow, Economic Education, the Mackinac Center for Public Policy (Midland, Michigan)

"*The Power of Agreement* is a well-written, reader-friendly book chock-full of practical wisdom and proven advice for effecting a positive, reality-based culture in any organization (large or small) whose leadership is serious about change. Author Brian Molitor is a seasoned veteran in change management and is one of the few experts that truly knows how to build a team. The concepts in his book can change the destiny of those in business, health care, government, or ministry! Brian is a man worth listening to. He won't waste a minute of your time in this book."

—Dr. Joel Freeman, director, the Freeman Institute; author; chaplain, Washington Wizards (NBA); and international conference speaker

"If the principles that are taught in this book were adhered to by government leaders, the existence of mistrust and cynicism toward our public officials would be virtually nil. I appreciate Brian Molitor's biblical approach in dealing justly and honestly with people. True success in everyday life is establishing proper relationships with people and taking the time to build and nurture those relationships. Brian Molitor is right on point!"

—Honorable Senator Mike Goschka (Michigan)

"In *The Power of Agreement,* Brian Molitor illustrates powerfully and articulately how the personal values that have guided his successful career can be applied in practical ways to the interpersonal relationships that are at the heart of business issues of all types."

—Richard Hazleton, chief executive officer, Dow Corning Corporation

"Congratulations to Brian Molitor for having the insight and courage to identify the key element in successful organizational change: productive relationships among people, created through trust, shared values, and open communication. Molitor illustrates his user-friendly framework with personal experiences and case histories. A good read—a good reference."

—Dr. Rushworth M. Kidder, president, Institute for Global Ethics

"*The Power of Agreement* is multidimensional in its approach and helps governments, businesses, ministries, family members, and individuals who desire positive change. Brian's wisdom is portrayed in his writings to us all. He holds nothing back. His book is a fresh approach written in novel style, which will hold your attention throughout. Implementation of these concepts have brought my business new dimensions of success. It is possibly one of the most profound books in this time period when change is the order of the day."

—Trevor Knoesen, owner and managing consultant, Productivity Improvement Consulting (South Africa), and owner and president, Pacific Rim Consulting (Hawaii)

"This easy-to-read guide will improve any organization's bottom-line performance. Speaking from years of experience and case studies, Molitor challenges you to accept change—when change is a challenge—and succeed."

—Peter Lowe, president and chief executive officer, Peter Lowe International, and founder, Peter Lowe's Success Seminars

"Molitor has given us an excellent, systematic process for building effective organizations and leading them through change. He builds on the foundation of vision, mission, and core values with practical operational steps any organization can implement. But this is not a cookbook of steps. It is an appeal to leaders to recognize that their success will come from caring about people and building strong interpersonal relationships."

—John E. Mulford, Ph.D., dean, Graduate School of Business, Regent University

"*The Power of Agreement* addresses two of the rarest but most essential success keys in the world today: unity and agreement. The discovery and application of these truths have been understood and experienced by the world's historic leaders. We need to rediscover and understand the major force that is buried in *The Power of Agreement.* The author of this book has an amazing ability to express deep truth and wisdom in a concise and effective way. The style of writing is exciting and vivid, which makes the truth stick in our memory. Brian D. Molitor is not presenting dry theory because the insights have been drawn from his deep well of experience in real life."

—Gunnar Olson, chairman, Alfapac (Sweden); chairman, AD 2000 business and professional network; and chairman and founder, International Christian Chamber of Commerce

"I have been associated with Brian Molitor for over six years now, and I am pleased that Brian was able to put into words his teachings and business practices that have been so inspirational in the growth and development of our organization. *The Power of Agreement* shows the beauty of balancing family, personal, and business relationships through the art of total and sincere communication."

—John Sivey, president, Wright-K Technology, Inc. (Michigan and Alabama)

"*The Power of Agreement* should be required reading for all industrial relations and MBA management courses. The book is easy to read, written in practical, down-to-earth everyday language. I felt as if Brian was talking to me! I know this book will be an instant hit!"

—Janet Victorson, Human Resources manager, Rhone-Poulenc, Institute Plant (West Virginia)

THE POWER OF AGREEMENT

BRIAN D. MOLITOR

BROADMAN & HOLMAN PUBLISHERS
Nashville, Tennessee

0-8054-1836-9

Published by Broadman & Holman Publishers, Nashville, Tennessee
Typesetting: Leslie Joslin, Gray, Tennessee

Dewey Decimal Classification: 658
Subject Heading: ORGANIZATIONAL CHANGE—MANAGEMENT
Library of Congress Card Catalog number: 98-48100

The story about Malden Mills on page 13 is the author's paraphrase of a December 1997 *Parade* magazine article. The source of the driver's license story on page 43 is the *Saginaw News,* February 1998.

Library of Congress Cataloging-in-Publication Data

Molitor, Brian D., 1952–
The power of agreement / Brian D. Molitor.
p. cm.
ISBN 0-8054-1836-9
1. Organizational change—Management. 2. Total quality management. 3. Interpersonal relations. I. Title.
HD58.8.M627 1999
658.4'063—dc21

98-48100
CIP

1 2 3 4 5 03 02 01 00 99

CONTENTS

PREFACE

This book was written to help organizations maximize their effectiveness and manage change by intentionally developing high quality relationships. It teaches a comprehensive approach to organizational development that is proven to be effective in business, industry, government, church, and family settings.

This approach was developed by Brian D. Molitor, the CEO of Molitor International, an international consulting and training company that he founded in the mid-1980s.

Practical in its approach, this book is supported by many on-the-job examples of the teaching points. It is written for leaders and followers alike who are interested in having their organizations achieve their greatest potential. It blends the best of today's organizational development techniques and a common-sense approach to human relations. The examples used are appropriate for an international audience, including readers in North America, Europe, Africa, and the Pacific Rim.

The title, *The Power of Agreement,* emphasizes that positive change within organizations comes only when two or more people agree on an issue, direction, project, or vision. The author hopes that this book will help many individuals make positive changes in their lives and build strong relationships with those around them.

Acknowledgments

I want to thank some special people for adding so much to my life and to this book.

First and foremost, I thank God for my precious wife, Kathleen. Your love and support are truly life sustaining. You are one in a million!

Thanks to my children—Daniel, Jenifer, Steven, and Christopher—for your love and patience. The joy that you bring to my life is beyond measure.

High on the list of special people are Bob and Ginny Molitor and Jim and Betty Hayes. Thanks for never giving up and for showing the way. Thanks, Joel and Tracy, for the early lessons on the power of agreement.

I am indebted to many faithful friends and associates who have sharpened, supported, and challenged me with their lives. At the top of the list are James Glenn, Harry Marcus, Ralph Cramton, Rick Suitor, Ron Ferguson, Marge Fredrickson, Shaenon Adamson, Karen Spickerman, Dr. Joel Robertson, Dr. Luis Gonzalez, Jan Clarkson, Gunnar Olson, Dale Neill, Charles Lange, Ralph Reed, Pastor Ron Ives, Linda Neuman, Trevor Knoesen, Kamal Bengougam, Dr. Joel Freeman, Burnett Kelly, Charlie Lacefield, Pastor Fred Smolchuck, Bill Parsons, Gene Klann, Cody Pelham, Bill Watkins, and Mark Holmes.

A special thanks goes to the fine people at Broadman & Holman who have worked so diligently to make this project a success: Lisa, Elizabeth, Paul, Len, and Bucky are the best.

Finally, I thank God who makes all things possible with his unconditional love, support, and wisdom.

PART 1

THE FOUNDATIONS OF CHANGE

CHAPTER 1

A TIME FOR CHANGE

CAUTION: *If you feel pain, faint, or dizzy, stop immediately.* These intimidating words are written on top of the exercise machine in my office. They subtly challenge my decision to get in better physical condition each time I step onto the machine for another torturous session. Often, midway through the workout, one word, *stop,* leaps out at me, and I am forced to decide if the future change is worth the present pain. Some days it is tempting to quit, but I know if I am to achieve my goals, I must keep working at it.

So it is for everyone who wants to make positive changes in his personal or professional life. The desire exists to have our nations, businesses, churches, and families achieve new levels of excellence. Change can be difficult, even painful. Yet, people worldwide recognize that it is time to begin managing change or risk very serious consequences.

Changes in political and trade philosophies result in amazing new alliances. A specific international example is the creation of the European Union and the North American Free Trade Agreement. Less dramatic, but just as significant, is the change in the world's approach to business. Global competition results in new business alliances seeking a competitive advantage. Quality has improved dramatically. Today's state-of-the-art product is tomorrow's reject—have you played any eight-track tapes lately?

Change is occurring in spiritual settings as well. Church growth and attendance are increasing significantly as people look to the heavens to find a purpose beyond personal profit.

As the unprecedented rate of change in our world continues, most people are simply swept along in its wake. Their destinies are decided by the decisions of others. Many try unproductive strategies when confronted by change. Some try to ignore change; others try to avoid it; still others try to resist or even sabotage it.

Fortunately, a unique group is emerging with the courage and wisdom not only to manage, but even to initiate change. These are the leaders who devise new strategies that enable their organizations to prosper. Some are formal leaders with impressive titles like president, chief executive officer, or general manager. However, many are people whose ideas have been previously overlooked. Foundational level employees identify ways for their companies to remain competitive. Impoverished single mothers *find* ways to bring peace to gang-controlled neighborhoods. Grassroots leaders with sincere desires to serve their nation replace selfish career politicians. The future is being shaped by change agents who arise to challenge the status quo around them. Some are endowed with compelling vision, verbal eloquence, and magnetic charisma. Others are armed with only rock-solid character and faith in a better way.

However, no individual has the power to create and sustain a positive change effort alone. Virtually every significant change in society, politics, business, and religion follows a similar three-step scenario. First, individuals or groups develop new visions for their "organizations." Second, they communicate their visions to others who agree to follow them in the new direction. Third, leaders and followers bond to form effective teams committed to seeing the new visions or changes accomplished.

A unique group of people is emerging with the courage and wisdom not only to manage, but even to initiate change.

While history tells the story of dynamic leaders who brought about great changes in the world, the key ingredient that helped them succeed often has been overlooked. That is, *agreement.* British statesman Sir Winston Churchill, businessman Lee Iacocca, King David of ancient Israel, American president Abraham Lincoln, India's Mahatma Ghandi, civil rights champion Martin Luther King Jr., the "Iron Lady" Margaret Thatcher, and Jesus Christ were leaders who shook the foundations of their worlds. In each case, they built teams of committed followers who took these visions for change seriously and sacrificially worked to turn their visions into reality. Each leader was a great communicator. Each understood that it took many people working together to bring about positive change. Each realized the importance of unleashing the dynamic, self-generating power of a team of people who have *agreed* to pursue a new vision. They will be remembered as victors despite the fact that each experienced suffering, opposition, and what seemed like defeat along the way. They must have heard the word *stop* during their trials. Yet, rather than submit to the tyranny of known limitations, they pushed forward into new freedoms. Some people today view these change-masters as heroes; others may disagree with their visions. All, however, must accept the fact that they had a significant impact on their worlds. They made a difference.

This book was written to assist people who feel called to be champions of change. It seeks to inspire innovation, improvement, and growth in the great organizations and institutions of our world. It is designed to give an understanding of the change process and help develop a team of people who are ready to release the power necessary for making positive changes in our world. That is *the power of agreement.*

QUESTIONS AND REFLECTIONS

Business • Government • Ministry • Family • Personal

1. What areas of your life are undergoing significant change?

2. What is your typical reaction to change?

3. What areas of your life should or could be changed for the better?

4. What will result if these changes are made?

5. Who are your champions of change? How did they impact their worlds?

CHAPTER 2

THE QUEST FOR EXCELLENCE

In Search of Excellence, the early 1980s book on corporate success, sparked a new interest in the concept of excellence. The book profiled many organizations that had achieved superior results in bottom-line categories. Suddenly, business leaders everywhere were talking about excellence and looking for ways to improve their organizations. During this same time period, a similar term, *world class,* found its way into mission statements of thousands of organizations. Everyone from chief executive officers to secretaries questioned whether their performances really were their best. This introspection resulted in a tremendous amount of improvement in a wide variety of organizations, including manufacturing, education, and government. People everywhere awakened to the fact that they had customers demanding high-quality service. The race for excellence had begun, but not everyone would reach the finish line.

WORLD-CLASS TOILET PAPER?

For a while, it seemed that every organization claimed to have world-class products. Unfortunately, companies with substandard products and services were quick to claim world-class status as well. I have eaten what were proclaimed to be world-class hamburgers, ridden in world-class rental cars, and even encountered world-class industrial toilet paper. However, I can assure you that none of these products performed in a manner worthy of the title. Organizations cannot achieve excellence or world-class performance simply by claiming it in a slogan or advertisement.

Leaders quickly learned that one of the first steps leading to excellence or world-class status was to establish a clear definition and *agreement on* what *excellence* and *world class* meant to each member of their organizations. However, this is much more difficult than it sounds. A nation's leaders declare themselves to be world class because they have spent billions of dollars building their military forces, only to face a rebellion from citizens who have no jobs and little to eat. A world-class army is of little importance to a person with an empty stomach. Likewise, countless fathers pride themselves on their abilities to provide material wealth for their families, only to have their children reject them later in life. The reason? They defined excellence in completely different terms. To the children, a world-class father is one who provides the basic material needs for the family and still reserves plenty of time to talk to, play with, teach, and love his children.

The most effective way to obtain agreement on what the term *excellence* means is to subdivide the broad concept into components that are easy to understand and measure. In the business realm, this allows each employee to understand how his individual performance contributes to the company's success.

An organization must excel in three main categories to be legitimately labeled *world class:* multiple bottom-line indicators, organizational longevity, and relationships.

1. Multiple Bottom-Line Indicators

All organizations exist for a purpose. They create products, provide services, or, in some instances, they do both. Therefore, each organization, whether church, business, or government, has measurable bottom-line indicators of success. The following is a list of universal bottom-line indicators.

Customer Satisfaction. Every organization today must address the issue of customer satisfaction. A long-standing definition of *customer* is someone who buys goods or services. However, many business leaders today understand that unless they expand this narrow definition they soon will see their former customers buying goods and services from the competition.

A customer is a person, group, or organization that we serve not only with our products and services, but also with information, technical support, and leadership. Customers may be inside or outside our organization. With this broader view, we can even see our families as customers—requiring our time, attention, protection, and love. Individuals within our work environment become customers requiring information, materials, and support.

> *Leaders have learned that the people closest to a task are the experts and can help to analyze ways for productivity improvements.*

Everyone has a customer in one form or another. A nation's elected and appointed leaders supply a multitude of goods and services for the citizens of their country. The citizens are, in effect, customers since they depend on their leaders for protection, a fair legal system, and sound financial policy. In the same way, parents are the "suppliers" for their children. As any parent can attest, these little customers require both goods and services, especially in their early years.

Leaders in pursuit of excellence must understand two key customer concepts. First, each organization has formal and informal customers. Improved organizational performance comes only after these individuals, groups, or organizations have been identified clearly. Second, there needs to be a significant change of attitude toward the customer. Leaders must view customers as valuable allies or partners to be served, rather than just as sources of revenue, labor, or taxes. Especially in the business setting, I consider a customer anyone whom an organization *serves*. This includes the obvious purchasers of goods and products, but also employees, coworkers, and stockholders. We can carry this definition over into other types of organizations as well.

Quality Improvement. In the past few decades, the Japanese business community has unintentionally done a great service for the rest of the world. They set new standards for product quality with their innovative manufacturing techniques. To a large extent, this was due to their embrace of W. Edwards Deming's work on statistical methods of quality improvement. Their production of high-quality products, such as automobiles, televisions, and video electronic equipment, has enabled the Japanese to secure new customers—in some cases, entire markets. As a result, the rest of the world raced to catch up with the quality front-runners.

Quality improvement, like customer satisfaction, is relevant for any organization. All organizations exist for a purpose. Therefore, the organization's output can be evaluated in terms of its current standard of quality and also can be analyzed for quality improvement opportunities. For example, a school system interested in quality improvement can record test scores of its graduating seniors and then discover ways to raise future scores. Governments can develop a quality index for a wide variety of its services. Crime, infant survival rate, poverty, new business start-ups—all can be recorded and analyzed for improvement. The bottom line on the topic of quality improvement is simple: Any organization that tries to maintain the status quo will soon find itself obsolete.

Productivity Improvements. Productivity and quality have a unique relationship. While quality improvement seeks to make something better, productivity improvement seeks to make something faster, in larger quantities, or with fewer resources. Organizations that achieve the greatest gains in productivity are those that discover the value of employee or follower input into the planning, problem solving, and decision-making process. Often this input is given in formal structures called by many different names. These include employee empowerment groups, employee involvement teams, and quality improvement teams. Leaders have learned that the people closest to a task are the experts and can help analyze ways for productivity improvements. I have worked with many corporate productivity efforts and am always impressed by the innovations created by well-trained teams. Productivity often skyrockets when employees are given opportunities to make suggestions on workflow redesign, new raw material requirements, and improved work assignments.

Waste Reduction. The worldwide concern for environmental quality has focused attention on the broad topic of waste reduction. This ranges from toxic waste storage to recycling junk mail. Organizations interested in making a positive change in this area also must challenge their institutional enemies of status quo and precedent. "We have always done it that way!" is not an acceptable response to a question about waste reduction.

Managed Growth and Expansion. Wise leaders constantly watch for growth opportunities. They explore the impact of enlarging existing facilities, improving their customer service, adding new product lines, and/or diversifying. They must carefully manage this expansion to prevent destabilizing existing operations by causing the organization to compromise quality or profitability. One of our small corporate clients experienced a sustained growth rate of 20 percent per year. In less than three years, their workforce had ballooned to more than six hundred employees. The downside of the growth was they had nowhere to put so many people. Desks were everywhere. The telephone system was inadequate. Customer calls were routed throughout the growing office complex in vain attempts to locate the proper people. Management spent so much time determining whether it *could* continue to grow that it failed to consider whether it *should* continue to grow. Each organization should be evaluated regularly to see whether it has become stagnant, if opportunities for growth exist, or if expansion is occurring at an unhealthy pace.

Management spent so much time determining whether it could *continue to grow that it failed to consider whether it* should *continue to grow.*

Security. Today's world is filled with unpredictability. Many organizations are "downsizing," which is today's sanitized term for dismissing employees. Often, downsizing is handled so poorly that "dumbsizing" is a more accurate term. Banks are merging. Nations are changing. This results in a universal uneasiness for everyone, including employees, stockholders, and the general population. Leaders who are legitimately concerned about their followers' security and well-being are rewarded with excellent cooperation and productivity, even during the toughest times.

Aaron Feuerstein, CEO of Malden Mills, has experienced this firsthand. The fact that he was a fair man who genuinely cared for his employees did not go unnoticed by them. In December of 1995, a fire destroyed much of his textile manufacturing plant in Massachusetts. The fire threatened to put his three thousand employees out of work, but Feuerstein chose to keep what he called his "most valuable resources" on the payroll—at a cost of millions of dollars—while the factory was rebuilt.

Critics said that the Bible-quoting CEO was being sentimental in his approach to business. But the results proved otherwise. His acts of kindness were rewarded even during the initial crisis when some employees actually risked their lives to save one of the mill's manufacturing buildings. Within ten days of the blaze, the area was back in production using newly purchased equipment and just a few employees. The productivity achieved by this group was miraculous. The small manufacturing unit produced 130,000 yards of material before the fire and after the fire it increased to 230,000 yards! Clearly, concern for employees' security improved the bottom-line performance at Malden Mills, and will do so wherever such concern is demonstrated.

Competitiveness. The sum of bottom-line categories is competitiveness. With very few exceptions, each organization wants to be the best in its field and, therefore, competes against its peers. Nations compete for trading partners. Businesses compete for customers. Political groups compete for voter support, and so on. Leaders must remember this fact . . . or risk losing to another organization that is more competitive.

This vigilance is especially important to groups that are currently the best of the best. Why? Because others have seen their success and are making plans to dethrone them even now. Competitors are researching ways to improve methods of operation and will do everything possible to succeed. If, as in a long-distance race, the lead runner remains diligent and committed to his mission, it will be very difficult for any competitor to overtake him. Excellence, however, is more than just great performance in a few bottom-line categories, or even short-term success in all of them. Excellence must be viewed from a broader perspective.

2. Organizational Longevity

Organizational excellence is like a person's honor. It can only be truly evaluated over an extended period of time. I find it fascinating that 46 percent of the companies on the Fortune 500 list in 1980 were no longer on that list in 1991. Even more amazing is that more than half of those companies ceased to exist during the same time period. Perhaps we need to create new designations for our organizations. I would love to see office wall plaques that boast of "temporary excellence" or "short-term world class."

It is foolishness when an organization declares itself world class this year and next year closes its doors because of poor planning. Just as in a football game, it is impossible to determine the winner until the end of the final quarter. One team may have a commanding lead early in the contest, only to become overconfident and lose to a more determined opponent in the final seconds. This is why I believe that the terms *excellence* and *world class* should be reserved for those individuals, families, businesses, and nations that sustain superior performance for long periods of time.

It is foolishness when an organization declares itself world class this year and next year closes its doors because of poor planning.

We need to revolutionize our thinking if organizations are to achieve their maximum potential. Progress must be measured in years rather than quarters as many businesses currently do. This short-term thinking creates tremendous pressure on managers to pursue short-term results—often at the expense of long-term goals—just to appease stockholders. Equipment is often operated too long without repair. Employees and their managers are worked to exhaustion as product quality slips. These practices lead to anything but excellence.

True excellence is achieved when we plan, reward performance, create supplier and customer alliances, and reinvest in our organizations on a long-term basis.

3. Internal and External Relationships

Productive relationships are built upon mutual trust and respect, open communication, and a clear understanding of expectations. Today, business leaders are beginning to comprehend that excellent productivity comes from having healthy relationships with customers, suppliers, and employees alike. Many organizations have learned the hard way that they must relate well to all three groups if they are to enjoy long-term success. The company whose leaders work well with their supplier of raw materials and customers but treat employees improperly often will find productivity and/or quality declining. Another company whose leaders work well with suppliers and employees but fails to satisfy customers soon may be out of business.

As an organizational development consultant, I hear countless leaders say, "Our high-tech company is vastly different from any other" or "This is a government group, so we have nothing in common with the business world" or "We are a hospital, totally unlike other types of organizations." My response to these statements is that they are all in the business of *relationships*. Obviously, there are some unique properties in each organization, and they offer a wide variety of goods, services, and information. However, they also share much in common. Invariably, the success of each organization depends on how effectively it manages essential relationships.

I strongly believe that lack of focus on relationships is the number one limiting factor and, potentially, the fatal flaw in countless organizations. During training seminars I often ask employees to estimate the percentage of productivity that their organization is currently achieving. Amazingly, their responses often range from 30 to 50 percent. They explain that this lack of productivity comes primarily from *relationship* problems. To be specific, they cite ineffective leadership, internal competition, and poor communication as the causes of substandard performance. In these sad settings, leaders and followers fail to agree on the organization's purpose and direction, and, invariably, employees work against rather than with one another.

Our world is filled with underachieving businesses, governments, churches, and families despite having all the resources they need to succeed. New technology, innovative marketing plans, and electronic commerce will all shape how business is conducted in the new millennium. However, success *will* come when people build the high-quality relationships that are necessary to propel them to *excellence.*

QUESTIONS AND REFLECTIONS

Business • Government • Ministry • Family • Personal

1. Which organizations are you familiar with that produce excellent products and/or services?

2. How do these organizations produce excellence?

3. Which parts of your organization legitimately could be described as world class?

4. Within your organization, are interpersonal relationships excellent? Something less? What is the impact of the condition of these relationships?

5. Which parts of your organization could not be described legitimately as world class?

6. What needs to change for your organization to become world class?

CHAPTER 3

THE CHALLENGES AND HOW TO OVERCOME THEM

The bad news: It is hard to make things change . . . period. Change can be so unsettling that people often resist even positive changes. Each time leaders decide to make improvements in their nation, business, school, church, or family, they can expect to be challenged.

The good news: Fortunately, most of these challenges are predictable and can be overcome.

CHALLENGE 1: NATURAL RESISTANCE TO CHANGE

Mark Twain is credited with saying that the only person who appreciates change is a baby with a wet diaper. Twain's quote seems to confirm my long-held suspicion that the only people who enjoy surprises of any kind are young children. The rest of us are comfortable with life's routines and resist any change in our personal worlds. This tendency is so strongly entrenched that we often tolerate a bad situation rather than risk something new. I believe this is true because every significant change brings many unknowns, and fear of the unknown often has a paralyzing effect on the human will.

People work at jobs that barely supply enough income to meet their needs because they fear leaving the security of the known. As bizarre as it seems, women who stay married to abusive husbands often do so for the same reason—predictable misery is better than the uncertainties of change. Many people loudly complain about the condition of their personal lives, families, churches, businesses, or governments, yet fail to take the first step in the change process. This resistance to change is universal, but it can be overcome with a strategic plan and a great deal of hard work.

HOW TO OVERCOME THE NATURAL RESISTANCE TO CHANGE

Develop a Clear Vision of the Future. People agree to change when they see a clear, positive picture of what they can become and/or achieve. They must be convinced that the change will benefit them or someone for whom they care. Employees asked to put more quality into their products must be convinced that higher quality means greater job security for them. Citizens asked to contribute more of their personal finances to the tax base or to serve in a nation's military often need to be reminded that their sacrifices will benefit their children and grandchildren.

Identify the Cost of Not Changing. Along with the benefits of changing, the cost of not changing should be pointed out too. For many years, corporate management and their union counterparts have been warned about the need to work together to compete against other organizations that make similar products. Some have listened and risen to the competitive challenge. However, thousands of companies have gone out of business because they failed to heed the warnings. In effect, they did not understand the cost of *not* changing.

Discover the Power of a Plan. People need to see a realistic plan that details how the proposed change will be accomplished. The world is full of powerful concepts, ideas, and proposals; but without a plan, these are little more than dreams.

This need for a plan was proven to me in the early 1980s when I served as an organizational change consultant for a large chemical company. Corporate leaders had decided to implement a program for quality improvement at their manufacturing sites throughout the world. They wisely chose to embrace the work of W. Edwards Deming as the foundation for change. However, after several months of hard work and thousands of dollars spent on the initiative, they discovered that quality had not improved. We soon discovered what caused their lack of progress. Although the entire management team supported Deming's fourteen-point philosophy on quality, they had no *specific plan* for how to apply the philosophy to their daily work. Once a long-term improvement plan was developed and implemented, improvements soon were realized.

Address the Negative People. A principle of magnetism is that positive attracts negative. This principle can be applied to making positive changes in an organization. The moment that a new plan is suggested, it will be analyzed and criticized by others. Christopher Columbus, for example, announced that he planned an ocean voyage to discover a new world. He was promptly told that he and his crew would sail off the edge of the flat earth and be destroyed. That was hardly an encouraging endorsement of his plan! Similarly, a writer of children's books was told by twenty-three publishers that his work was unacceptable. The twenty-fourth publisher embraced his writings and promptly sold six million copies—the author was Dr. Seuss. We must become like Columbus, Dr. Seuss, and countless individuals through the ages who found the courage to pursue their dreams, despite their critics.

I have devised a simple strategy for dealing with negative people in an organizational setting. Whenever someone criticizes a developmental effort, I first make sure that the person understands what is happening and how it will affect his or her organization. If the person is still unreasonably negative after clarification, I challenge him or her with a few questions. What is their motivation for resisting the change process? What will he gain if the effort fails? If it succeeds?

Next, I ask whether the person has a better strategy for making positive change in the organization. If so, why hasn't his plan been implemented yet? After reflection, most people agree to observe the progress without resisting the efforts of people around them. Many of these doubters actually have become strong supporters of the process as it has moved forward.

There also comes a time for negative members of an organization to decide whether they truly want to remain there or move on to another opportunity. I have often heard well-meaning experts describe organizations as families. While some organizations have developed a family atmosphere, I am convinced that this description creates a great deal of confusion. A business, government, or even religious organization is described more accurately as a community than a family. Community implies choice, options, or consequences for actions more readily than family. If you are not happy in one community you can sell your property and simply move to another. However, you are born into a family and are forever related to your parents, siblings, and other family members. With this in mind and as a last resort, some negative employees need to be reminded that there is no blood bond linking them to the organization and they may be much happier in a different community.

Keep People Informed, Involved, and Encouraged. Resistance to change can be overcome by keeping people informed, involved, and encouraged. A friend of mine, Ron Ives, is the pastor of a church in Mount Pleasant, Michigan. He recently used this approach during a successful building program. In the initial phases, church leaders communicated the need for the new building with the congregation. Members of his small congregation soon were convinced of the need for the new facility, but they were somewhat skeptical about their ability to undertake the task. To overcome their fears, Pastor Ives held numerous meetings with the entire congregation to keep them informed of the plans and ask for their ideas on the building layout and other decisions. He further built support for the project by involving people in committees that were commissioned to study everything from sanctuary carpet color to bathroom decor. Church members did much of the actual construction work, too. Ron and other church leaders agreed to build the structure debt free and encouraged parishioners to apply principles of debt reduction in their personal lives.

Whenever the project stalled because of a lack of funds or other hindrances, Pastor Ives would remind the congregation of the original vision for the building. The new building would be a place to help the hurting people in the community, especially the many young people in need.

He also continued to encourage them with reports of the excellent progress that had been made to that point. No one was ever condemned for what had not been accomplished, only praised for what had been accomplished.

By using this approach to overcome resistance to change, members completed the new building debt free and without any lasting division in the congregation.

It is important to understand that it takes time to keep people updated on change. Often this is the very excuse given by leaders who are reluctant to keep their followers informed. They reason that they cannot afford to take time away from other more important issues just to talk with employees. My response to this shortsighted view is simple and blunt. They cannot afford *not* to take time to interact with their most valuable resources. Personal interaction between leaders and followers is the only sure method of transmitting the vision, mission, core values, and critical issues facing an organization.

The approach used by Pastor Ives can be used successfully in government, business, and family settings as well. First, share your vision with people and explain the need for the change. Then, keep them informed, involved, and encouraged along the way.

CHALLENGE 2: LACK OF TRUST

Positive change efforts often are hindered by a lack of trust. Politicians who make promises to their constituents and then fail to keep them are soon handicapped in their pursuit of progress. A husband who compromised his marriage vows in the past now has difficulty convincing his wife that he wants what is best for their family. Employees ignore their corporate officer's warnings of economic disaster. Why? They've heard the same words during times of prosperity and simply fail to believe that a real threat exists.

All too often politicians, government officials, corporate managers, and parents make promises without intending to fulfill them. The impact on those around them is profound. Trust and credibility are broken the instant that deception or dishonesty surfaces. It is important to realize that people are usually long on memory and short on forgiveness when someone has deceived them.

This also creates a "guilt by association" mentality that can have long-lasting effects. For this reason, a leader who desires to make significant change in an organization should know the record of his predecessors. They may have been liars, coldhearted tyrants, incompetent, or, simply, people who were solely interested in their own career advancement. This type of individual makes short-term plans that benefit himself without concern for the long-term impact on others. Until the new leader proves that he is different, those around him will likely assume that he is like their former leader.

When I was growing up, my father bought a beautiful Siberian Husky for a family pet. The dog's previous owner had labeled it as "impossible to train" and "stupid." When we brought the dog home, it reacted strangely when my father approached it. Although my dad tried to be kind to our new friend, each time he raised his hand to pet the dog, it would growl fiercely and slink away. We quickly realized that the previous owner's labels were better suited to himself than the dog. His method of "training" the dog was obviously violent, and the dog assumed that its new owner would treat it the same way. After months of consistent kindness, my father was able to win the trust of the dog.

It is important to realize that people are usually long on memory and short on forgiveness when someone has deceived them.

When confronted with new leaders who have plans for change, people often act just like our pet. They growl or hide until convinced that what is happening is in their best interests. As they move in a new direction, effective leaders patiently wait for their followers to develop trust.

Another condition that creates mistrust in relationships—and therefore slows an organization's ability to change—is inconsistency. Inconsistency can mean disaster for an organization when policies, protocol, and personalities change without warning. The father who returns home from work each day and lovingly greets his wife and children will always find his personal welcoming committee waiting at his door. They have learned that his arrival will be a good experience. His family trusts him because his behavior is predictable.

In contrast, the father who is kind to his family one day but abusive the next soon finds no one waiting to greet him. Why? Because he is inconsistent, and therefore unpredictable. His family has learned that the potential reward of his blessing is not worth the risk of his wrath. They don't trust him.

In the same way, the president of a nation who constantly changes his position on such issues as capital punishment, inflationary policies, and taxation soon will find that he has lost credibility with his citizens. The lesson here is simple: To be trusted, your actions must be consistent and predictable.

As corporate consultants, my associates and I have interviewed thousands of employees throughout the world. These face-to-face interviews reveal amazing truths about the power of personal relationships. We have learned that businesses that experience the greatest difficulties with change have one thing in common: their leaders have little personal contact with workers. In these settings, managers and supervisors give employees general directions and provide the basic necessities for them to do their jobs. Other than that, workers rarely see management except when there is trouble. Employees get a tremendous amount of negative attention when a problem occurs. Bosses flood the problem area and work feverishly until it is resolved. Once the problem is resolved, these "leaders" disappear until the next mishap.

During one assessment, I asked a group of employees if they trusted their managers. They simply replied no. Expecting to hear some examples of extreme mismanagement or scandal, I asked additional questions to clarify reasons for the mistrust. I was amazed to learn that the employees had never been abused or lied to by their leaders. One member of the group captured the reason for their lack of confidence in leadership in this simple statement: "How can we trust someone we don't know?"

HOW TO OVERCOME THE LACK OF TRUST

Communicate, Communicate, Communicate! After many years of flying on commercial flights, I have decided that there are two kinds of airline pilots: good and bad. This has little to do with their ability to safely fly an airplane, but much to do with their ability to communicate with passengers concerned about flight connections, getting to meetings on time, or returning home after a long trip. On routine flights, a pilot's announcements provide some assurance that all is well. Pilots cover the basics, such as whether you are on the proper plane going to the correct airport. But when the routine changes, such as a delay or bad weather, good pilots talk to passengers to calm their fears. Few situations are more frustrating than sitting in a cramped airplane for an extended period with no idea of what is happening. A quiet pilot simply compounds the passenger's frustration.

The same is true with organizational change efforts. Nothing is more frustrating for those involved than to feel that their lives are about to be changed but they don't know how. Honest communication is the best way to overcome mistrust and calm fears.

Remember that the remedy here is not just communication, but *honest* communication. I experienced a memorable example of the difference during the take-off of a transcontinental flight. Our plane had begun accelerating down the runway when we heard a loud boom that came from the starboard engine. Instantly, passengers screamed, prayed, and prepared to evacuate the plane as we slowed to stop. Time seemed to stand still as we waited for the worst to happen.

Two hundred and fifty passengers breathed a collective sigh of relief when we began to taxi back toward the terminal. Since this was the last flight of the night, I began to make plans for the unexpected stay in Washington, D.C.

I was amazed when our plane returned to the start of the runway instead of to the terminal. We all were looking around nervously when the voice of the pilot came through the speakers. Trying to sound confident, he announced that, "We had a slight problem with our starboard engine, but it seems to have cleared itself up. So we'll be on our way."

I quickly ran through a mental list of things that "clear themselves up." I came up with the common cold and minor arguments with my wife, but nowhere on my list was a problem with the starboard engine of a jumbo jet. By the grace of God, we took off on the next try and eventually landed safely at our destination. The pilot had tried his best to calm our fears with his announcement, but he failed. Why? As seasoned travelers, we knew that his message was not completely honest. Communication without honesty is just propaganda. People will recognize it, so don't bother.

To overcome a lack of trust you must be a "good pilot" and honestly inform people concerning what is about to happen in your organization. Tell them where you are going, how long it will take, and what they can expect along the way. Everyone will appreciate the journey much more.

Check for Complete Understanding. When communicating, it is vital to be sure listeners understand the message and to be sure that all of the information presented has been received accurately. Unfortunately, a large percentage of what is said, written, and/or announced in the corporate world is lost before it reaches its intended audiences.

Not long ago, I experimented with a group of managers to see how effectively they transferred vital information about their organization to their subordinates. Their company held monthly meetings attended by all managers above the level of first-line supervisor. Each month's agenda was filled with presentations about company policies, compensation, new regulations, and challenges to their corporate survival. Presenters used the latest technology to transmit information to their peers. They used jazzy laptop computers, multicolored overhead transparencies, and a multitude of carefully collated paper handouts. Generally speaking, the presenters were well organized and thorough. They spoke skillfully about a wide array of data points, starting dates, and decisions that would have significant impact on the lives of their colleagues. Following the meeting, the managers in attendance were expected to share the information with their subordinates.

My experiment was simple. One month, I asked the meeting moderator for five minutes to address the managers at the end of the presentations. I handed out a blank sheet of paper to each manager and asked them to write all the significant items they had heard during the previous two and one-half hours. I made it clear that they were to focus on information that would have special impact on their subordinate's work or personal lives. After all 120 managers had finished writing, I collected the sheets and returned to my office to review them.

What I discovered confirmed my earlier suspicions. In terms of important information, some managers got most, most got some, and some got none. A few of the sheets were filled with detailed information that subordinates needed. Some sheets were blank, and the majority contained a few words or incomplete sentences that related to topics shared during the meeting. This meant that a great deal of the information the group was to have learned had somehow disappeared. What is so amazing is that this loss of information occurred *before* the managers had even left the room. Imagine how much more was lost once they had returned to ringing phones, beeping computers, and the hectic pace of the day.

The impact of this communication breakdown was predictable. Employees felt devalued and demotivated because they did not receive relevant information about their workplace. As a result, they rarely took any initiative to make decisions and often complained that their bosses did not care about them. It is important to remember that the managers in this company meant well and were investing a great deal of time—and money—in the meetings to try to foster good communication. They just failed to ensure that their people walked away with the vital information that was presented.

We remedied the situation in future meetings by developing a "teaching points" approach to each person's presentation. We asked all presenters to supplement their presentations with a single-page handout. This sheet outlined the specific points that were vital for the listeners to understand and take with them. Our new approach helped presenters focus their information on the most crucial points and, therefore, saved a lot of time in the process. Using the handouts exponentially increased the transfer and retention rate of information throughout the organization. Soon, employees began to feel more a part of the team and were equipped with information necessary to make good decisions.

Build Personal Relationships. An outdated management philosophy encourages leaders to remain distant from their subordinates. Just as in old military settings, fraternizing with subordinates is not permitted. It was feared that too many interactions between leaders and followers would breed contempt for leaders and cause the entire operation to collapse in anarchy. Promoters of this autocratic management style believe that rules and regulations, rewards and punishment are the primary tools for successful leadership. Perhaps this is true for maximum security prison guards and lion tamers, but the rest of us would do well to learn another way.

The other way is as simple as applying the Golden Rule to working relationships. When we treat people as we would like to be treated, our lives become so much simpler. We can dispense with the political games, manipulation, and silly ego trips that so many people allow to become part of their work lives. With very few exceptions, the people around us simply want to be treated with respect, kindness, and professionalism—the same as we do. We must take time to get to know them and understand their strengths and weaknesses, goals and dreams, worries and fears, so we can relate to them properly. Strong personal relationships are keys to building workplace unity and commitment.

Does this approach come with some inherent risks? Certainly! Will anyone ever try to take advantage of the situation? Of course! However, as leaders, we often jeopardize our working relationships with 98 percent of our coworkers in order to guard ourselves against the 2 percent who may try to take advantage of us. I prefer to establish policies, procedures, and relationships that encourage the majority rather than control the minority. In this type of positive work environment, negative people soon are either converted or, because they find the openness so uncomfortable, they leave.

Share Common Goals, Interests, and Challenges. It is human nature for us to uncover our differences with others before we discover what we have in common. Often, work relationships are much like the phenomenon of continental drift, where giant landmasses slowly pull away from each other. It takes real work for people to comprehend that they have much more in common than in conflict. We often forget that people come to work for the same basic reasons. At the most foundational level, we work to earn a paycheck, health benefits, and security for our families. Once these basic needs are met, work becomes a place where we enjoy a sense of purpose and an outlet for our creativity.

The human side of the equation is equally important. We often find that leaders, coworkers, and customers value our contributions, which adds to our self-esteem. We can develop a sense of camaraderie with coworkers, which meets our need for community relationships. This short list gives us more than enough in common to begin building solid relationships where we work. Also, it is amazing how many common interests people share within a workplace. The majority of our lives revolve around our families, faith, recreational activities, sporting events, children's achievements, and personal growth and development. Any and all of these topics can be the basis for conversation and, ultimately, enhanced workplace relationships. Common challenges also can create strong relationships within the work environment. New competition, potential for job loss, and stricter government regulations all can be the basis for coworkers unifying their efforts and their relationships.

CHALLENGE 3: RELUCTANCE TO CHANGE BECAUSE OF PAST FAILURES

"We tried that before and it didn't work." We often hear this statement when someone suggests a change of any kind. Whether it involves empowering corporate employees or reconciling a broken marriage, someone will whine these infamous words. What these doubters overlook is that, although the statement may be true, it fails to recognize one of the greatest qualities of the human race: We have an innate ability to learn, grow, and change.

Today we can analyze yesterday's defeats and turn them into tomorrow's victories. The husband who sincerely desires to make his marriage work after several failed attempts will probably succeed. Why? Because he has experienced the pain of loneliness and his heart demands another try. He has checked his priorities and now sees value in the family that he once ignored. He has sought wise counselors, read books on the subject of marriage, and learned to manage his time, money, and other resources in order to accomplish his goals. He has changed. Personal pain is an unpleasant teacher, but an effective one.

The same principle holds true for a company, church, or nation that has stumbled in the past, but is now committed to making positive change. They can learn. They can grow. They can change.

One of the greatest qualities of the human race: We have an innate ability to learn, grow, and change.

I am reluctant to hire anyone who claims to have never made any serious mistakes. Those people are either so timid that they never attempted anything greater than their known abilities, or they are liars. I prefer to share my work with those who have been bruised in their quests for excellence. It is a joy to join forces with those who refuse to accept the status quo as a way of life for their family, business, church, or nation. The survivors of these expeditions into uncharted territory use their mistakes as mileposts on the way to understanding and success.

We desperately need to free ourselves from the shackles of past mistakes when we begin to change our organizations. In one sense, we need to become like children again, to rekindle the wonderful quality of faith in things that we cannot see. As children, the first time we tried to walk, we fell. Yet, how did we react? We weren't content to crawl for the rest of our lives just because our first attempts at walking had failed. Instead, we got up and tried again until we succeeded.

One of our corporate clients had tried to implement six major developmental programs in six years. None succeeded in making any significant improvement. I was asked to identify reasons for the lack of success. A thorough analysis showed that in each case, upper management had made some serious mistakes. While they spoke in glowing terms about each new program, management failed to commit sufficient time and/or finances to allow the change to occur.

I then worked with management to design a new approach that took into account mistakes of the past. When we announced to the employees that another attempt at change was forthcoming, the reaction was predictable. The most vocal people tried to derail the effort with discouraging comments like, "It will never work," "The people here just don't care," and "This is the same old stuff." Fortunately, this organization's leaders responded like children learning to walk. They got up and tried again. The results were astounding! Productivity and quality went up. Customer complaints and employee grievances went down. They overcame the past.

HOW TO OVERCOME PAST FAILURES

The Two-Pronged Approach. Leaders must use a two-pronged strategy to overcome the pessimistic power of past mistakes. First, they must be convinced that their new direction is right and that they have acquired the information, technology, finances, and/or political support necessary to avoid another failure. The second part of the strategy involves communicating this information to followers in a convincing manner. Often, this includes acknowledging the problems of the past and apologizing when appropriate.

One of our corporate clients recently demonstrated how powerful this concept could be. This unionized company of six hundred employees had a long history of labor-management strife. As we worked with leaders of management and the union to find ways to work more cooperatively, we found it difficult to make any real progress. The reason? Everyone seemed to be stuck in the past.

Management kept detailed records of all errors and shop rule violations made by employees over the years. Union employees kept their own unofficial records of management transgressions. The most senior managers and employees served as tribal elders who kept the stories of the other group's misdeeds alive. Each believed it was his duty to warn newly hired employees about the rival tribe, which could never be trusted. Whenever anyone tried to suggest a new way of working together, the ideas were drowned in a flood of negative comments about the past. The results of our assessment questionnaire revealed an amazing truth. The stories of past misdeeds had taken on a life of their own. The worst offenders from either side were no longer even employed there! When confronted with this reality, leaders on both sides began to explore ways of building on what they shared in common.

Clean Slate Day. After a year of extensive training in interpersonal relations, the culture of the organization began to change. During the second year of the change effort, the plant manager initiated a unique program that he called Clean Slate Day. He assembled all six hundred employees and announced that he had purged their records of all negative reports. In an unprecedented move, he gave each employee a completely clean slate regarding disciplinary actions and even poor performance records. In return, he asked union employees to give the current managers and supervisors a clean slate of their past misdeeds as well. In effect, he asked each person to forgive past mistakes and forge a new working relationship built on trust and common goals. As an outward symbol of the new commitment to change, he proposed that managers discard their white hard hats and employees discard their blue hard hats.

Next, the plant manager announced that he had purchased six hundred gold-colored hard hats and had them placed by the exit doors of the meeting room. At the end of his presentation, he extended both a challenge and an exhortation to each person. Those who were truly ready to forgive and forget the past and embrace a better future were to leave their old hard hats and pick up new gold ones as they left the room. The response was overwhelming. When the last employee left the meeting, only three gold hard hats remained unclaimed. Since that time, the organization has grown and prospered as never before. The plant manager had found a way to break from the past and create the organizational agreement necessary to succeed.

CHALLENGE 4: FEAR OF POWER LOSS

Most of us enjoy power, position, and authority, and the status symbols that go with them. We expend massive amounts of effort in our quest to progress up whichever ladder we happen to be on. A business executive works seventy-five hours each week to attain a higher position. Politicians redraw the boundaries of their districts to increase their influence. Young married couples sometimes spend all their spare time working to gain the status symbols of a new car and big house. Since so much of our identity is found in the positions that we hold or the things that we possess, we should not be surprised by how we resist any change that might cause us to "lose" whatever power and control we have gained.

Evidence that we intensely resist changes that threaten our personal power is everywhere. We are much like Phileas Fogg, central figure in the classic novel *Around the World in Eighty Days*. He demanded that every clock in his home be set at exactly the same time and lived his entire life according to an unchanging schedule. An enraged Mr. Fogg even dismissed his butler because he failed to keep his bath water at a precise temperature. Now *that* is resistance to change! This obsessive eighteenth-century nobleman has many modern counterparts. Middle managers and supervisors unsure of their abilities to adjust to an empowered work environment often vocally denounce a proposed program of labor-management cooperation. Why? They fear that their power bases will be lost if they begin to cooperate with the "other side."

HOW TO OVERCOME THE FEAR OF POWER LOSS

Explain the Need for the Change. Often this resistance to change comes not from misguided malcontents or pitiless power mongers, but from faithful members of our organizations who honestly believe that the change will negatively impact their lives. I have learned that most of these people are glad to work with their leaders to create new, meaningful positions for themselves in the organization if given the opportunity.

It is also important to teach people the difference between positional power and power of influence. Job titles and positions may be changed, but our true power comes from the ability to influence others positively. When this is clearly understood by leaders and followers alike, an organization can make many changes without a great deal of resistance.

It is unfortunate, but some changes will have a negative impact on some people. In today's world of downsizing, outsourcing, dismissals, and program cuts, many jobs are changed significantly or eliminated. Leaders have a moral obligation to find comparable jobs for all displaced employees whenever possible.

Resistance or Rebellion? To overcome the fear of power loss, leaders must understand the difference between resistance and rebellion. The former may be tolerated, but the latter must be eliminated. Sincere resisters are won over by honest discussion about the need for change, its impact on their lives, and attempts to minimize any losses they may experience because of the change. Many of our corporate clients have successfully used displaced managers and supervisors as schedulers, researchers, or salespersons. This has produced dividends in two ways. First, they have retained some of their most valuable people, rather than releasing them to another organization. Second, others correctly interpret this as a sign of the organization's commitment to all employees, who usually respond with excellent performance for years to come.

Those people who are rebellious are an entirely different matter. They oppose—even sabotage—change efforts for strictly selfish reasons. Once it is clear that an individual is vigorously opposing change without a valid reason, that person must be dealt with. It is the organization's responsibility to help influence resistant individuals by providing training, coaching, counseling, and/or transferring them to another position if one is available. If, however, an individual chooses to continue negative activities, he should be dismissed.

To optimize our organizations, we must reward workers who demonstrate maturity regarding the use of power. Some organizations have people who refuse to let go of their power or position for any reason. They continue to operate as they choose, no matter what is said to them. I have learned the hard way that this type of person will not get better with time. In fact, if not corrected, they tend to become worse and will pull many others down to their level.

This was demonstrated clearly in an employee empowerment program we helped to implement at a company in the southeastern United States. Our initial assessment revealed most supervisors and middle managers used a dictatorial management style. One manager in particular, Joe, was extremely bad. He insulted, threatened, even cursed at employees under his "care." He was an icon of old-style management. Whenever top managers confronted Joe about his actions, he would call a cease-fire for a few days but return soon to his abusive management style. This pattern repeated itself many times during a three-year period.

As the rest of the organization grew and matured, Joe got worse. The longer his poor conduct was allowed to continue, the bolder he got. He began to influence other supervisors to ignore their leader's vision of a cooperative workplace, encouraging them to regain "control" of the workforce.

Three years after our project with this company began, we conducted a series of follow-up assessment interviews with fourteen hundred union employees who revealed a powerful truth. The issue that was foremost in their minds was Joe's negative behavior! This despite the fact that the organization had a significantly improved bottom-line performance, had built a new $50-million production unit, added forty-four new union jobs, and the vast majority of managers were treating workers better than ever. Employees bitterly complained that Joe was making a mockery of the change process. The employees correctly reasoned that if top management was serious about long-term change, they should offer Joe early retirement or simply dismiss him because of poor performance.

Unfortunately, they did neither. Top management missed a golden opportunity to forge an inseparable partnership with the union and other employees. Rather than exercising their options to either move Joe to another nonsupervisory position, retire, or fire him, they did nothing. Their refusal to confront Joe's rebellion literally stopped progress at that company. The employees refused to go any further under those conditions. The lesson here is simple: Do not allow rebellion to destroy the vision. Teach true principles of leadership and openly condemn power mongers.

CHALLENGE 5: CONFLICTING PROGRAMS, POLICIES, AND ACTIVITIES

By its very nature, change conflicts with existing programs, policies, and activities. Change is conflict. Change efforts also compete for limited resources. People, finances, technology, information, and time are required to implement even the simplest new initiative. Visionaries who attempt to change their organizations are often told by others that the new idea is too expensive or too time consuming to implement. Often, the exact opposite is true. The organization simply cannot afford *not* to change.

My wife and I regularly discuss goals for improvement in our home. Through the years, we have focused on many issues, such as developing the talents of our four children, spending more quality time together, and slowing down the hectic pace of life. On occasion, we find that we are trying to accomplish two goals that are in direct conflict. We recently discovered that we had scheduled too many activities for the children in too short a time period. The constant driving to piano lessons, karate classes, and football games frustrated us. These activities were in direct conflict with our goal of spending more quality time together. It wasn't until we had a family meeting to clarify our priorities and resolve the conflicts that "relative" peace returned to our home.

Several years ago, a company called us to help them develop teamwork among their employees. During our initial meeting, they inadvertently shared secret plans to lay off 25 percent of the workforce in the coming months. They hoped that a training program would pacify their employees while many of their coworkers lost their jobs. My associates and I quickly ended the meeting and left. These hypocritical leaders were trying to implement two programs with conflicting philosophies at the same time. The outcome was predictable and would have been disastrous.

Problems can occur even with initiatives that are properly aligned philosophically. Often this happens when organizations try to do too much with limited resources. We seem to forget that all new initiatives are subject to the limitations of finances, time, and the ability of the people around us to adjust to change.

One of our manufacturing clients was suffering from the dreaded trying-to-do-too-much-with-too-little disease. They tried to implement several programs to improve performance. Although each program had excellent potential, failure was inevitable. Why? Each program competed for finances, human resources, and even meeting rooms. To make matters worse, a different manager, each trying to rally other employees to his cause, championed each program. The results were chaotic.

Multiple, disjointed programs create an illusion of progress, but, in reality, they create only problems.

Staff meetings became evangelistic appeals in which managers preached the virtues of their programs and subtly condemned the others. This divided the employees into several hard-core factions that wanted little to do with their unenlightened counterparts. Top management once tried to end the destructive competition by requiring all middle managers to attend every meeting that was announced. I visited this company several months after this decision was made and was shocked at what I saw. The middle managers seemed to be suffering from a form of corporate battle fatigue. They shuffled their feet as they went from one meeting to the next. Their eyes were red from lack of sleep as they worked sixteen hours each day for weeks at a time just to keep up with the schedule. Their family relationships were strained. Quality suffered as abandoned employees were left to make management decisions on their own.

Only one of the company's original initiatives received enthusiastic support from employees, but with a very ironic twist.

A few corporate managers, far removed from the realities of the workplace, dreamed up a voluntary separation program for the plant. These masterminds hoped to reduce its already Spartan workforce by approximately seventy-five employees. Some older employees would retire early with full benefits while some younger employees would receive a full year's salary to find work elsewhere. The perfect plan, right? Wrong! The managers were shocked when six times that number flooded the personnel office eager to leave all of the turmoil at work. Entire departments applied to leave at one time, which threatened the company's very existence.

Eventually, top management had to withdraw its offer to many employees who had made plans to leave. This dropped the dismal morale even lower. Management finally agreed to end all but the highest priority programs, but by that time, a great deal of damage had been done.

How to Overcome Conflicting Programs, Policies, and Activities

The lesson here is simple. *Develop a long-term plan—and follow it!* Multiple, disjointed programs create an illusion of progress, but, in reality, they create only problems. To avoid the headaches that come with conflicting programs, decide first which of the current initiatives are essential. Nonessential ones must be discarded or placed in hibernation until a more appropriate season. Finally, develop a long-term, comprehensive plan that includes your current methods of operation and top priority change initiatives, yet leaves some room for unexpected demands on your organization's resources.

CHALLENGE 6: LACK OF PATIENCE

Our world is filled with fast food and fax machines. Supersonic aircraft shuttle us between continents in just a few hours. We surf through dozens of television channels in seconds. Merchants are open for business twenty-four hours a day, seven days a week, so customers can shop whenever they please. Throughout the world, credit card debt has grown exponentially. People gladly use their cards to get what they want now and pay for it later, accepting, perhaps as a form of penance, the high rate of interest added to their bills each month. However, high interest rates are not the only downside to all of our high-speed convenience and instant gratification. We become easily frustrated when we have to wait for anything.

I confess that when I go to restaurants I hate waiting for soup to cool. It just takes too long. Sometimes I think that the cooks see me coming and turn their scalding cauldrons up another hundred degrees or so. Perhaps the waiters are in on the plot as well. They seem delighted to deliver the dish to my table quickly. Once served, I typically wait no more than fifteen seconds and then just dig in despite the steam swirling off the surface of the soup. The result of this folly is always the same: a severely burned tongue, which causes more delay than if I had waited longer in the first place.

Impatience is often promoted by the world around us. We constantly are confronted by advertisements promising smaller waistlines, clearer complexions, and higher IQs in three weeks or less. In reality, our waistlines get smaller with a serious commitment of time, exercise, and—unfortunately—fewer desserts. In the same way, we cannot expect to change a business, city, or nation without a long-term plan of action. We must not be like advertisers who promise rapid results without personal sacrifice or patient endurance.

It is interesting to hear the campaign speeches of a presidential candidate. Faithful followers cheer as they hear a new vision for their nation. Expectations rise with each promise of lower taxes, safer streets, and better schools. Millions of people are motivated to vote for the candidate, sometimes resulting in a landslide victory. But a strange thing happens six months later in office. The president, so loudly cheered as a candidate, is now labeled ineffective, or worse yet, a liar, because the campaign promises have not materialized. Why? The citizens are impatient and, to some degree, ignorant of how long it takes to change even a single policy, let alone an entire nation. Change takes time in our personal lives. In our professional lives, change takes even longer because of the number of people involved.

HOW TO OVERCOME THE LACK OF PATIENCE

Keep the Vision in Sight. Several years ago, a woman in England achieved her vision of obtaining her driver's license. What made this accomplishment so noteworthy is that it had taken her twenty-seven years, ten instructors, eighteen hundred driving lessons, and nearly thirty thousand dollars in fees to achieve it. It seems she had difficulty remembering which pedal was the brake and which was the clutch. This caused her to plow through a construction site during one driving test. Her instructor was not amused. During a later test, she became nervous as a police car approached her from the rear, sirens blaring and lights flashing. She had the presence of mind to pull over to let the officer pass. Unfortunately, she picked the wrong direction and pulled directly in front of the police car. Neither the policeman nor her instructor was amused.

There is a happy ending to this story. At the age of forty-five, she was finally granted her license. Her response to the examiner was, "Are you sure?"

Like this persistent woman, we must keep our vision in sight if we are to avoid the problem of impatience. The athlete who dreams of competing in the Olympics can endure the pain of preparation by picturing herself standing on the winner's platform as her national anthem is played. An entrepreneur working twelve hours each day in his own business is motivated by the hope of financial independence. A nation's president in the midst of turmoil is strengthened by the vision of his country's future peace and prosperity. The vision produces patience because of its promise of a better future.

Consistent Communication. Leaders help develop patience in their followers by clearly communicating the vision, expected benefits, and realistic timelines involved in the change process. This creates a sense of well-being in the followers and keeps them involved in the process of growth and development. Leaders who fail to keep their followers informed soon find their organizations filled with fear, dissension, and resistance to change. The first step in every successful organizational development process is to communicate clearly with everyone involved about the vision, plan of action, and probable impact on the operation. Ideally, these issues are communicated to each level of an organization through face-to-face presentations rather than some type of posted bulletin or printed memo.

Leaders must provide opportunities for dialogue and sufficient time for people to ask questions about each phase of the proposed developmental effort. When people understand that change is a long-term process, they tend to relax and carry on with life. If they expect instant results, it is an entirely different story. Like children hungrily hounding their mother for a cake to come out of the oven, they will not be satisfied until the change is "done." For example, much of our work involves the development of leadership skills in managers, administrators, or government officials. The process of learning and applying these new skills does not occur overnight; rather, change happens over an extended period of time. Therefore, we try to establish and communicate realistic timelines to leaders and their followers *before* any training starts.

Unfortunately, we learned about the need for this the hard way. Years ago, we spent little time doing this type of pre-training communication. It seemed like wasted time. Instead, we got right to work holding training classes for a company's leaders. This raised a very high—and unrealistic—level of expectation in leaders and followers alike. They somehow had the false belief that several days of training would result in perfection for each attendee. These newly trained supervisors and managers returned to find employees waiting to pounce on the smallest mistake. We soon learned that time spent in up-front communication was anything but wasted. We changed our approach to create more realistic expectations for everyone involved. This new approach results in increased leader perseverance, follower patience, and, ultimately, the success of the effort.

CHALLENGE 7: LACK OF LEADERSHIP COMMITMENT

This challenge is the most difficult to understand and the most damaging to an organization's growth and development. Leadership commitment is vital, especially in the early stages of change. Leaders initiate most of the action and keep the process moving forward by their commitment of time, money, support, counsel, and other resources.

In the late 1980s I had the task of implementing a quality improvement program in an automobile parts plant where the leader's lack of commitment to change was obvious. Early in the process, I attended a meeting in which the plant manager told his workforce about the importance of quality and safety in the workplace. Although he used all of the proper words, his employees were uninspired by his speech. A quick tour of the plant revealed the reason for their indifference. The machines were all relics made in the 1940s. They were incredibly loud and virtually impossible to adjust for quality improvement. They spewed oil like mechanical volcanoes. Some enterprising employees made canopies from pieces of scrap cardboard to protect themselves from the constant shower of oil coming from overhead lines. The plant had no automated system for handling materials, which meant that employees had to carry each piece of razor sharp sheet metal from one machine to the next. It was easy to identify the long-term employees by the number of scars on their hands and arms.

The impact of this work environment on the company's bottom line was predictable. The company suffered from low levels of productivity, quality, and profitability. Further evidence of the chaos were high rates of absenteeism, employee turnover, grievances, and injuries. Customer complaints were common since error and rework delayed most product deliveries. How did the plant manager respond to this situation? He gave lectures to employees on the need for *them* to build quality into *their* products. He scolded *them* for *their* lack of productivity and threatened *them* with job loss if *they* did not improve. All the while, the plant manager refused to invest the funds necessary to upgrade the machinery, provide safety equipment, and clean up the plant. Obviously, he was not sincerely committed to improving his organization, and his speeches could not convince the employees otherwise.

Another incredible example of this leadership commitment problem comes from a manufacturing company in the western United States. Their most profitable product was rubber tubing used in surgical procedures. The company's primary customer called late one Friday afternoon pleading with the production manager to build additional products immediately. The manager promised the customer that the plant would work throughout the weekend and ship the parts on Monday morning. He then went to his workers and made an impassioned plea for them to sacrifice their weekend pursuits in order to keep the customer satisfied.

Everyone was told to be at the plant at 7:00 A.M. the following morning to begin an emergency production run. The employees canceled weekend plans and dutifully arrived the next day only to find the doors locked. They assumed that their manager was running late and sat down on the sidewalk for the brief wait. The brief wait turned into a real test of their devotion to the company. At about 9:00 A.M., the production manager finally pulled up in front of the employees, hopped out of his sporty convertible, and unlocked the doors to the building. He offered neither an apology nor an explanation for his late arrival.

Incredibly, as soon as the employees began to work, he informed them that he had another commitment that prevented him from staying for the production run. He then sternly stressed that he expected them to have the products ready by the end of the day. Before any of them could respond, he quickly returned to his car and drove away. His casual clothing and the golf clubs plainly visible in the back seat of his car left no doubt that his other "commitment" was waiting at the local golf course. The faithful employees finished the job by day's end, but they resolved never to be fooled again by the manager's speeches about commitment.

HOW TO OVERCOME THE LACK OF LEADERSHIP COMMITMENT

Count the Cost—Burn the Ships. Leaders must be convinced themselves that their vision is valid and can be accomplished. Next comes a solid plan, complete with timelines. Wisdom demands that they now acquire sufficient resources to carry out the plan. Once this is completed, they then must build a coalition of other leaders and followers to help achieve the vision. Finally, with all of this in place, they must pursue the vision with the tenacity of a tiger until it is completed.

It is crucial to understand that if leaders show anything less than complete confidence in and commitment to the vision, then the support of followers will falter and eventually die. When the Spanish explorer Cortez landed on the shores of what is now Mexico, he made sure that the men accompanying him understood that they must succeed. In perhaps the ultimate show of commitment, he burned the ships that had brought them, ensuring that they would succeed . . . or perish in pursuit of their vision.

Most of us won't find it necessary to burn anything to show our commitment to our visions. However, in pursuit of the vision we should be prepared to sacrifice at least as much as our followers do. I believe that a sacred responsibility comes with every position of leadership. Fathers and mothers, ministers and managers, presidents and kings all must understand that they are to do everything in their power to lead followers safely through to the end. It is the height of hypocrisy for a leader to speak as if the vision is the ultimate, only to act as if it is irrelevant. Leaders who demonstrate their commitment by both words and deeds will have a multitude of willing supporters to accompany them on the journeys.

QUESTIONS AND REFLECTIONS

Business • Government • Ministry • Family • Personal

1. How do you react to change? Why?

2. How does your organization respond to change and new ideas?

3. What lessons did you learn from past attempts at positive change that succeeded?

4. What lessons did you learn from past attempts at positive change that failed?

5. What is the greatest obstacle to positive change in your organization or personal life?

6. How can the obstacle be overcome?

Chapter 4

TRADITIONAL APPROACHES TO CHANGE

One of the necessary evils in life for those of us over the age of forty is the annual physical examination. Some of you can identify with me. Much of the doctor's exam might be considered atrocities if done by enemy soldiers during a time of war. Once the assault on body and dignity has ended, we anxiously wait for the results. Consider our reaction when the doctor speaks those dreaded words: "You need to lose a few pounds." We go into shock at the thought of dieting and immediately drive to the nearest restaurant to consume the richest dessert on the menu, then we begin to formulate our quick weight-loss plan. It is human nature to resist change; but when change is unavoidable, we want to make it as quickly and easily as possible. When the doctor advises us to lose weight for health reasons, we have two choices.

First, we can choose the quickest "program" approach possible. As soon as we finish our dessert, we can call our local hospital and sign up for a liposuction procedure. We actually can pay a surgeon to lance our bodies in various spots and invade our "innards" with a stainless steel vacuum cleaner. This will remove pounds of fat instantly—we can figure out what to do with all the extra skin later. For those of us who think this procedure is too radical, we can find another method to shorten the process of change. We can join a health club, begin to exercise seven days a week, and try the latest fad diet that promises weight loss in record time by eating tree bark and dirt.

While these approaches may result in some short-term weight loss, they are condemned to fail in the long run. Why? Because they are based on procedures and programs that cannot be sustained. Liposuction, crash diets, and extreme exercise programs all fail to address the foundational issues that caused the weight gain in the first place. These short-term events are not substitutes for a sustainable change in lifestyle.

A much better approach is to gradually change our eating habits and commit to some form of mild exercise three times a week. Within a year, we will permanently lose the unwanted pounds and see some significant improvements in our health. The type of change that lasts begins with a completely honest evaluation of our current conditions. It ends with the subsequent changes of our foundational habits, values, patterns of behavior, and even our relationships with others.

THE PROBLEM WITH PROGRAMS

A program, by definition, has a distinct beginning and ending. Many attempts at change in business, government, and religious organizations are similar to the format of a television program. The program begins at 8:00 P.M. with a great deal of fanfare and shows previews of the exciting scenes to follow. At 9 :00 P.M. the program ends, often leaving the viewers wondering why they wasted an hour of their lives on something so trivial. In business, the program often begins with a passionate proclamation from company leaders about the need to change. They declare that quality must be improved, and pledge their deep commitment to this new focus. More quality control employees are added to the staff. Posters with catchy quality slogans like, "Quality Is Everyone's Job" and "We Love Our Customers" appear everywhere. Top management is seen in the work areas daily. For a short time, quality actually may improve. But, as with all programs, it soon ends.

Employees begin a poster campaign of their own. The bathroom walls and inner-office memos contain revised slogans like "Quality Is No One's *Job" and "We* Loathe *Our Customers."*

Corporate management begins to complain about the increased cost of the new employees' salaries, so they are dismissed. The remaining employees observe that, despite all of their rhetoric, management is still willing to ship substandard goods to customers to maintain constant cash flow. Soon, employees begin a poster campaign of their own. The bathroom walls and inner-office memos contain revised slogans like "Quality Is *No One's* Job" and "We *Loathe* Our Customers." When the program is finally over, only one thing has really changed: Management has lost credibility with employees and customers alike because they tried to use a program rather than a comprehensive process for change.

IS IT A PROGRAM OR A PROCESS?

Each year hundreds of companies announce that they are entering a new era of quality, profitability, or customer service. After each election, national leaders declare that the day of selfish government is over, and a new day of concern for the citizens has begun. Is there any way to know which of these initiatives will prosper? In the early stages of any change effort, it is difficult to tell whether the effort will become a new way of life or simply fade away. However, the following indicators determine whether the effort has been designed as a short-term program or as a long-term developmental process.

LOW LEVELS OF INVOLVEMENT

One of the most telling indicators is the amount of involvement people have in the change process. A manufacturing group that sincerely desires to improve its product quality must involve its quality producers, the employees, in the planning process. The national leader who tries to mandate change without truly understanding the issues of primary importance to his citizens will never rule securely. The reason? People often ignore, resist, or even sabotage new programs that they didn't help create. Without a sense of ownership, we tend to view any new idea from a distance, asking, "What is in this for me?"

I often ask my workshop participants whether they wash a rental car before returning it. Their answer is always the same: no. Their rationale? They don't wash them because they don't own them. They will pay to use them and will try to avoid damaging the vehicles, but their concerns end there.

Many fathers have suffered self-inflicted agony when they violated this principle of involvement. A classic example is when a dad plans the family vacation around activities and locations that he prefers, while ignoring the wishes of his wife and children. The trip of his dreams soon becomes a nightmare of endurance as he pretends to enjoy himself amidst the complaints of his children and icy stares of his wife.

The lesson here is simple: If you fail to involve the people around you in the planning and implementation of any significant undertaking, you will find yourself having to do all of the work and still falling far short of your intended goal.

THE CRISIS OR FAD OF THE MONTH

Hold it! This month's figures are in. Productivity dropped, rejects increased, quality slipped, someone filed a grievance. Are these causes for concern? Of course they are. Are these causes for a drastic change program to be implemented? Of course they are *not.* But many organizations have started major initiatives when one of these "crises" occurred. Often improvement programs are conceived by well-meaning individuals who really don't understand the process of change. A crisis-of-the-month program is usually suggested by the Chicken Littles of the world. In the classic American children's story, Chicken Little is a neurotic baby chick that gets hit on the head by a falling acorn and promptly begins to run through its world squawking, "The sky is falling!" Too often, a change program is started because of an isolated problem or temporary crisis.

We must learn to study trends to see whether the "crisis" is only a normal short-term variation in the standard. Similar to this is the fad-of-the-month program promoted by leaders who approach organizational development like ice cream salesmen. They offer a different flavor each month. One month the special is safety, and the next month it's quality. They even boast about the large variety of flavors (programs) that have been offered in the recent past. Unfortunately, these new programs are quickly discarded and replaced by new ones. Obviously, neither the crisis nor the fad approach makes much sense. Each results in short-term programs with few long-term gains for the organization. There is a tragic by-product of these approaches to change. In time, employees view the very topics that should become integral parts of an organization as trivial additions.

The following topics are often pursued by leaders who chase the latest crisis or fad. Although each concept has the ability to improve an organization, none has the power to transform it *by itself.*

Motivation. A leader who selects motivation as a primary organizational development strategy assumes a great deal. Specifically, he assumes that the people involved have everything they need to be productive and efficient, that interpersonal relationships are optimal, and the only component missing is motivation. This is a classic crisis program topic. Organizations often bring in motivational speakers, such as professional athletes, to inspire employees. Their speeches can be exciting, and sometimes motivating. But they generally provide a short-term caffeine-type boost that wears off and may leave people feeling worse than before the speech. The reason is simple. As soon as the thrill of the speech fades, employees realize that the problems that demotivated them still exist. They lose all sense of motivation when they realize that their leaders have failed once again to take *action* to resolve the real issues.

Employee Suggestion Programs. The age-old concept of an employee suggestion box is a good one. However, it should not be the primary means of gathering employee ideas. These efforts are often plagued with problems. For example, many of the suggestions have not been researched to confirm their feasibility. This creates additional work for managers and supervisors who may not have the time to spare. In the worst-case scenario, suggestions may be stolen from the person who submitted them, causing distrust and employee apathy.

Occasionally, suggestion programs reward quantity rather than quality. As a new employee in a large factory in the late 1970s, I was amazed at our company's suggestion program. It promised to reward anyone who submitted ten suggestions at any time during the year. I quickly learned that the other employees ignored the program for most of the year and then submitted their ten suggestions just before the December 15 deadline. The corporate offices would be flooded with thousands of suggestions, most of which were worthless. One senior coworker was a master of this system and proudly showed me a copy of his suggestions. They included such novel ideas as cutting holes in the roof to let the hot air out in the summer and drilling holes in the floor to drain away any water that comes in through the holes in the roof. Just before Christmas, the company would present the employees with a turkey as their reward—which seemed strangely appropriate. Clearly, there is a need to obtain suggestions from followers, but there is a better way to handle the process, as we will explore in the next chapter.

New Organizational Structures and Reporting Relationships. Organizations often need to restructure and change reporting relationships to optimize performance. However, executives who are most successful do what is necessary to prepare their workforce, customers, and managers *before* the restructuring takes place. Also, it is folly for a company, government, or school system to develop a new structure without first clearly identifying problems that indicate such a change is necessary.

One of our clients, a small firm that had one hundred employees, experienced perennial problems with low product quality and high employee turnover. Two individuals who shared the top management responsibilities owned this company. One was in charge of production, the other in charge of sales and marketing. Their method of dealing with their company's shortcomings was unique. Approximately every two years, they would exchange jobs. In some strange way, they saw this as progress; but their workforce saw it for what it really was—a useless exercise that ignored the real problems plaguing the organization. They finally decided to make some foundational changes in their operation and have since begun to prosper.

Quality Promotion. Organization leaders are finally learning the importance of quality in their goods and services. This revelation has led to numerous quality improvement programs in business, education, government, and health care operations. These programs go by many different names: total quality management, quality improvement programs, and statistical process control programs. While this new quality revolution is exciting, its leaders often find themselves fighting the battles for improvement by themselves. It takes all members of an organization working together to achieve true quality improvement. This lifestyle change can be built only upon high quality relationships throughout the entire organization. Only companies that understand the human side of the quality equation can reach and sustain new levels of quality in their products and services.

Productivity Incentives. For years, business leaders have tried to motivate employees to be more productive by offering financial incentives for each completed unit of production. This has, at times, encouraged additional production, but often at the expense of quality.

Employees have always been quick to learn ways to beat the system. I recall a coworker who was responsible for operating an industrial laser in an automotive assembly plant. He was required to place a power steering housing into a machine, push two buttons to run the laser inside of the housing, remove the housing, and repeat the process hundreds of times each day. Each time he pushed the buttons, a counter on his machine would advance, crediting him with one completed unit of production. On days that he was particularly upset with the department supervisor, my coworker would modify his production routine slightly. He would simply leave the housing in his machine and run the laser over and over again inside the same part. This did three things: First, since his pay was partially based on his production, he received money for work that he did not do. Second, it created a headache for the plant managers who could never figure out what happened to all of those extra parts that appeared on the monthly production run sheets. Third, it compromised the quality of the parts that were run through the process multiple times. Productivity incentives can be beneficial, but only when there is an honest and mutual labor-management commitment.

Efficiency Improvement. Every organization should look for ways to be more efficient. Often, it is helpful to have someone from the outside identify blind spots that may be missed by those close to the situation. However, misuse of this practice comes when outsiders are invited in for a few quick observations and then allowed to make recommendations to dismantle entire components of the operation, lay off employees, or change the organization's basic mission. Too often, "efficiency" experts recommend staff cuts rather than additions and fail to spend sufficient time with local personnel to truly understand the complex issues that face the organization.

TWO FAULTY ASSUMPTIONS

All too often, leaders make two faulty assumptions when they attempt to implement a new program.

Faulty assumption #1—The People Understand the Reason Why Change Is Needed and How It Will Benefit Those Involved.

Unless elements of a program are explained in detail *before* it begins, the people involved will not understand—and may even resist—the effort. Production managers have failed miserably in their attempts to have employees monitor output with statistical process control charts. Why? Management failed to communicate how the initiative could improve product quality and customer satisfaction, thereby providing job security for the employees.

Many leaders have learned to use this concept to their advantage. For example, some insightful managers in charge of airport construction projects communicate the need for changes to passengers *before* passengers began to complain. They put signs at airport entrances saying, "Please excuse our mess, we are expanding our facilities to better serve you." This accomplishes two things. Initially, it defuses the potential anger of travelers by acknowledging the inconvenience. It also explains in simple terms that the purpose for the construction is to improve customer service. Remember, people confronted with change are much more likely to support it if they receive an honest and timely explanation about the change.

Faulty Assumption #2—The Organization's Interpersonal Relationships Are Strong Enough to Sustain the Strain of Change.

Leaders often discount the role that emotions play in organizational effectiveness. Employee emotions are never neutral. They always have either a positive or negative impact upon the change process. Invariably, leaders who fail to comprehend this suffer severe consequences for their lack of perception. I have witnessed this many times in a variety of organizations.

For example, hospital employees in Department A have a good relationship with their supervisor and are generally satisfied with working conditions and compensation. Their sense of physical and emotional well-being causes them to respond with happiness, commitment, gratitude, and hard work. In this setting, the employees' work performances are outstanding.

However, at some point their supervisor is replaced with a new one who "cracks the whip" and wants to shape up the department with lots of changes. She doesn't fraternize with employees because she believes if she does, they'll take advantage of her. What is the employees' emotional response to the new work environment created by their supervisor? Predictably, it is anger, bitterness, apathy, and inattention to details. Their work performances falter and quality slips. Soon it is obvious that the changes aren't working.

At this point, top management may notice the performance problems and may try to train employees to do better work. They shouldn't bother. The real issue that needs to be addressed centers on negative employee emotions and poor relationships. Failure to recognize this condemns management to a long, hard process of change and relegates employees to disinterested spectators.

Presidents, managers, and parents who fail to build productive relationships with followers always fall short in their quest for excellence.

We must remember that communication, cooperation, and personal productivity are directly linked to the quality of our relationships with those around us. Organizations with weak interpersonal relationships always struggle with change. While it is usually the top leaders who initiate change, it takes committed people at all levels to accomplish the change successfully. Presidents, managers, and parents who fail to build productive relationships with their followers fall short in their quest for excellence. This is why it is so critical for leaders to understand the power of agreement.

QUESTIONS AND REFLECTIONS

Business • Government • Ministry • Family • Personal

1. Have you ever tried the quick-fix approach to change? What were the results?

2. Are you familiar with organizations that fail to involve employees in planning and implementing change efforts? What are the results?

3. Are you familiar with organizations that try the "flavor" or "crisis of the month" approach to change? What are the results of these approaches?

4. Are you familiar with organizations that try to achieve excellence with new organizational structures and/or reporting relationships? What are the results?

5. In your organization, do people understand the need for change?

6. In your organization, are the interpersonal relationships strong enough to withstand the strain of change? How can they be strengthened?

Chapter 5

SOLID FOUNDATIONS FOR CHANGE

Some of the most significant changes in my life happened just after I reached thirty years of age. Set in my ways, I was living the normal life of a single man in the beautiful state of Michigan. For me, normal life was trout fishing in the spring, relaxing in the summer, deer hunting in the fall, and hibernating in the winter. My work experiences up to that time were diverse and unique. I had spent time as a union factory worker, manufacturing plant supervisor, lumberjack, semiprofessional football player, and residential youth camp director on an island in the middle of Lake Michigan.

Even my approach to education was nontraditional. Working as a bouncer in a raucous rock-and-roll bar funded my masters degree program at Central Michigan University. Although my lifestyle was disjointed and even somewhat self-destructive, it had become comfortable for me. Like so many people, I was content just drifting along wherever the river of life would take me. I wasn't all that resistant to change—I just had never taken the time to consider that anything *should* be changed.

During a rare quiet moment, I began to think about life differently. I realized that some of life's best opportunities were passing me by and that something was missing. Like so many companies today, I wanted to change but was unsure where to begin.

THE REAL MISSING LINKS

Although organizations try to manage change, growth, and development in various ways, many attempts at improvement fall short of their goals. Now let's discover the missing components and learn how to apply them.

Both individuals and organizations alike need more than a quick-change program to reach their optimum levels of performance. They need a complete renewal, from top to bottom. This type of change begins the instant a new vision is conceived. It takes shape as the mission, goals, and priorities are clarified. In organizations, it gains momentum when people rally around a set of core values and operating principles that allow them to act as individuals but succeed as a team. People and organizations that sustain the momentum of change long enough for it to become a way of life always include three components in their change-process design. These missing links are high quality relationships, high levels of involvement, and commitment to a long-term process.

HIGH QUALITY RELATIONSHIPS

Positive change cannot be dictated, mandated, or forced upon people. It must be presented in a way that creates a desire for change in the hearts of those impacted by the initiative. Positive change occurs fastest and most efficiently in an atmosphere of trust and openness. Ideally, leaders are sure of where they are going and truly care about those who follow them. Followers must trust both the competence and character of their leaders before they will embrace change without reservation.

Therefore, high quality relationships are the foundation of every successful change effort. Wise leaders understand the need for connecting with those around them before undertaking a significant change effort.

Mature leaders realize that they can't suceed by themselves, despite society's constant barrage of messages to the contrary. Through the years, popular songs have captured the world's self-centered approach to life and success. Musical hits like "I Did It My Way" and "I Gotta Be Me" may be entertaining, but they aren't very accurate. In this life, there is not much that happens without the help and support of others. And it is virtually impossible to gain this kind of support on a long-term basis without developing and maintaining productive relationships. I am not referring to some kind of bizarre corporate brotherhood where employees all hold hands and sing the company song to get motivated for work every morning. Neither am I suggesting that our organizations *de*volve into bizarre encounter groups that collectively check their biorhythms before coming to consensus on what color to paint the company rest rooms. I am saying that the quality of the interpersonal relationships in an organization plays an immense role in the organization's ultimate success or failure.

The most common cause of low organizational effectiveness is poor interpersonal relations. Fortunately, it is also one of the easiest issues to address. Unfortunately, this area often is overlooked in the search for improved performance—with disastrous results. Our corporate leaders are often too busy to see what is so glaringly obvious. Strong personal relationships are the foundation for successful families, businesses, and nations—period. Conversely, weak personal relationships quickly cause these same entities to crumble and fall.

These simple truths have application for us as members of organizations and as individuals. One of the first things that I recognized during my time of self-reflection was that all of the relationships in my life were superficial. I couldn't honestly claim a close relationship with God, family, coworkers, or friends. That is a dangerous place for anyone to be, and yet it is precisely where many people, especially leaders, find themselves. Today, we often lack support from our families because we spend so much of our waking time working. Friendships are often shallow for the same reason. The climb to the top of the corporate, government, or religious organization is a lonely one as we overwork to impress our leaders, compete against our peers, and have little time to fraternize with our subordinates. This causes many of us to feel isolated, even when we are part of a large organization.

In the corporate world, leaders often have a stronger relationship with their work than with their workers. It is common for managers, supervisors, and administrators to know what their followers have been assigned to *do,* but little about who they *are*. Followers know even less about their leaders. In these situations, tasks have become more important than relationships. Sadly, leaders who spend little time on relationships never obtain their followers' full commitments to change. I have seen hundreds of worthwhile projects in businesses, churches, educational institutions, and governments fail for that one reason. Unproductive relationships have created a culture in which trust, commitment, and agreement are absent. People in these organizations expend just enough energy to maintain the status quo, but no more. Shortsighted leaders who overlook the importance of strong relationships condemn their organizations to failure, often without knowing why.

America's automotive manufacturing giants and their satellite industries have tried for years to implement improvement programs, but with limited positive impact. Why? Poor labor-management relationships, mistrust, and an unwillingness from employees to change.

If you are a glutton for punishment, ask a veteran union worker from a General Motors plant about the *Quality of Work Life* program that was attempted in the 1980s. The initial program concept was a good one with admirable goals. It was supposed to increase worker involvement, boost productivity, and instill a greater sense of ownership in the organization for all employees. With few exceptions, employees who endured a *Quality of Work Life* program tell a woeful tale of millions of dollars spent and countless hours wasted with little positive return.

The program eventually was put out of its misery when labor leaders withdrew from continued involvement. The interpersonal relationships were not strong enough to withstand the inevitable problems that accompany this type of effort. The massive size of a manufacturing giant like General Motors (GM) provides some short-term protection against the problems caused by poor relationships; however, size can only prolong the inevitable.

The disagreements between GM and the United Auto Workers (UAW) union became obvious to the world when a strike crippled production during the summer of 1998. The UAW chose to strike at some key parts plants rather than organize a nationwide strike. This strategic move effectively shut down GM's operations while minimizing the union's financial exposure. The cost to GM was a staggering 1.2 billion dollars in second-quarter profits alone! Clearly, the leaders of GM and the UAW treated each other as the enemy before and during contract negotiations and acted accordingly. To think that they will begin to cooperate following this type of traumatic event is folly. The battle lines in the corporate world are clearly drawn and, as in every war, there will be no winners—just survivors.

The lesson here is plain. We must stop viewing organizations with a charts-and-graphs mentality. We must begin to see organizations more from a human perspective. Regardless of what type of organization you belong to, you are in the *people* business. Despite the addition of new technology, computers, and robotics, an organization's success or failure will always depend on human factors. Governments, businesses, churches, and hospitals depend on people at every level for their very existence. People supply these organizations with raw materials. People make their products and provide services. People must attract other people who will use or purchase the goods and services, and so on. It is all about people. Organizations achieve maximum prosperity only as long as the interpersonal relationships among their people remain productive.

I enjoy helping companies with work process reengineering projects. The problem-solving ideas really flow when a group of people brainstorms how to make an organization more productive. In these sessions, we cover entire walls with large sheets of paper detailing every step in a particular work process. Using this reengineering approach, we are able to see the original design and theory of how the organization is to function. But we would miss a crucial reality if we stopped there. I am convinced that for any reengineering project to succeed, we must put faces and names in the boxes on the organizational charts. I encourage leaders of every organization to invest time in statistical analysis of their work processes, time/motion studies, identification of bottlenecks, and so forth. However, I also encourage leaders to add the human element to their studies.

It is only in theory that we can design or redesign a perfect work process. For example, in theory, automobile assembly line employee 1 performs his job and passes the automotive component to employee 2, who, in turn, performs his particular function on the component, passes the completed part to employee 3, and so on. When the last step has been accomplished, a flawless automobile is ready for dealer delivery. Pretty simple, right? Not exactly.

Not every automobile that makes it to the dealer is flawless. I should know, I bought one of them. What causes defects, errors and flaws? In some cases, it is poor-quality raw materials and defective components. However, quality problems often come from the human side of the equation.

What the assembly line work flow diagram shows is employee 1 passing completed work to employee 2. What the diagram doesn't show is the condition of the relationship between the two employees. Neither does it explain the condition of the relationship between them and their supervisor. I have interviewed numerous employees who confessed to sending substandard or incomplete work to the next employee as a way to get even with that employee for some unresolved conflict. Others have boasted that they intentionally left parts out of production components, virtually guaranteeing a defective final product. The reason? Their supervisor had given them a hard time in the past and this was, in their words, "pay-back time."

The message here is clear. We must spend as much time reengineering our workplace relationships as we do our work processes. Then the reengineering theory becomes reality and we are able to change the organization. Using this process, we determine the competence, commitment, and condition of key relationships affecting every individual involved in the work process. We then can discover if a technical design flaw, poor raw materials, human error, or a breakdown in relationships among the people involved causes a problem. An otherwise flawless work process design can be ruined by poor communication between leaders and followers or by some unresolved conflict among employees.

HIGH LEVELS OF INVOLVEMENT

In today's world, terms like *involvement* and *empowerment* are discussed often, but seldom understood. We seem to have a difficult time finding balance on this issue. In the name of involvement, some well-meaning leaders try to delegate virtually all decision-making to their followers. Regardless of the leader's motivation, this approach is obviously wrong. One of the primary responsibilities of leadership is to make high-level decisions about the direction of their organization. Leaders cannot abdicate this responsibility or delegate it to followers.

A similar problem arises when leaders mistakenly believe that they themselves must make *all* of the decisions that impact their organization. This practice forces other members of the organization to assume robot-like roles of doers instead of thinkers. All too often, meetings are held to discuss major changes in family, church, business, and government settings without the proper people attending. Often, leaders, without any follower involvement, make decisions about complex subjects that will profoundly impact their organizations. Corporate downsizing and new product introductions send shock waves through a workplace, and yet these are often implemented without any worker involvement up front. Handled this way, meetings may be quick and easy, but also deeply flawed. I know of a previously thriving church that split into two antagonistic groups because its members were not allowed to give their views on the color of the sanctuary's new carpet. We must remember that virtually every decision to change an organization will require some degree of follower support to make the change succeed. One of the most important lessons of change for leaders to understand comes in the following saying: *Meaningful involvement creates support and commitment.*

If an initiative needs support and commitment from followers to succeed, then it is vital to involve them early and often in the design and implementation process. The reason for the high levels of involvement is simple, yet compelling. People support what they help create. We tend to take care of things that are ours. Remember, we don't wash rental vehicles for one fundamental reason: We don't own them.

Production employees know more ways to build quality into a particular product than their corporate managers ever will. When given the opportunity to contribute their ideas, employees make sure that their products are the best possible. Every sincere attempt to involve and empower followers will eventually succeed. I have witnessed employee problem-solving groups discover millions of dollars of cost savings for their companies. Imagine how much government bureaucrats could learn by communicating directly with the citizens whom they represent. Our nations will be much more productive, and citizen commitment will skyrocket once the people are truly part of the decision-making process. It is important to remember that involving followers in making decisions is much more than an attempt by leaders to be nice. It is a precise strategy for enhanced performance and increased competitiveness. Involved followers are more committed to the mission and will sacrifice to see it accomplished.

Commitment to a Long-Term Process

As I mentioned at the start of this chapter, my life began to change dramatically in the early 1980s. The catalyst for some of the biggest changes occurred when I was married at the age of thirty-one. Though it may seem a bit old-fashioned, my wife and I made vows to remain together *forever*. Our vows were not made to sustain our commitment during only the honeymoon. That was the easy part. They were made for the tests and trials that regularly assault every marriage once the honeymoon has ended. We saw marriage as a life-long journey, not a two-year contract with renewable options that so many couples seem to favor today. We planned for our relationship to be a marathon, not a sprint.

Soon after the wedding, many other exciting changes occurred in my life. The next decade saw a restoration of relationships with my extended family, a new relationship with God, new business opportunities, and the birth of our four children. Each change required a deep, long-term commitment on my part to realize fully their benefits in my life, especially during times of adversity. In the first few years I questioned whether I could be a world-class husband and father—especially once the children came along. There was little time for my beloved trout fishing trips, and "relaxing" meant five minutes alone in the bathroom. There is a temptation for anyone—and any organization—going through change to reflect on the good old days . . . and perhaps want to return to them. I am glad that I didn't go back. Whatever sacrifices I may have made are nothing compared to the joy that my family brings to me.

So it is with our businesses, ministries, governments, and other organizations. Without commitment to a long-term plan, change efforts quickly falter. At the first sign of trouble, someone will want to quit and return to the good old days. They completely forget that if the old days had been so good, the change would not have been initiated in the first place.

At the first sign of trouble, someone will want to quit and return to the good old days. They completely forget that if the old days had been so good, the change would not have been initiated in the first place.

Remember that the long-term approach to change is like a marriage: The people involved make unbreakable vows of commitment to each other. This commitment represents a new and better way of life for everyone involved without the option of turning back. In an organizational setting, the long-term commitment ensures follow-through on the change process regardless of the challenges.

In part 1 of this book, we have laid a foundation for change. Also, we have explored the challenges to change and some strategies to overcome those challenges. The bottom line is that high quality relationships are the foundation on which all successful change processes are built. Now in part 2 we will discover the foundation for managing change and learn how to develop those relationships that propel our organizations to peak performance.

QUESTIONS AND REFLECTIONS

Business • Government • Ministry • Family • Personal

1. Would you describe the relationships among those in your organization as productive? Why or why not?

2. What is the impact of the current condition of interpersonal relationships on your organization's future?

3. Do people feel that they are meaningful parts of your organization? How are they involved?

4. Does your organization have long-term plans for change? Does everyone understand them?

5. Are there areas of your personal life that you would like to change? What currently prevents you from doing so? How can you overcome these challenges?

PART II

THE MOLITOR DEVELOPMENTAL PROCESS

The following chapters explore the process of change. Also, they provide case studies of organizations that have changed successfully. The chart that follows shows the primary components in the process and how they relate to one another. Each component on the chart is explained in detail in the chapter listed below it.

THE MOLITOR DEVELOPMENTAL PROCESS

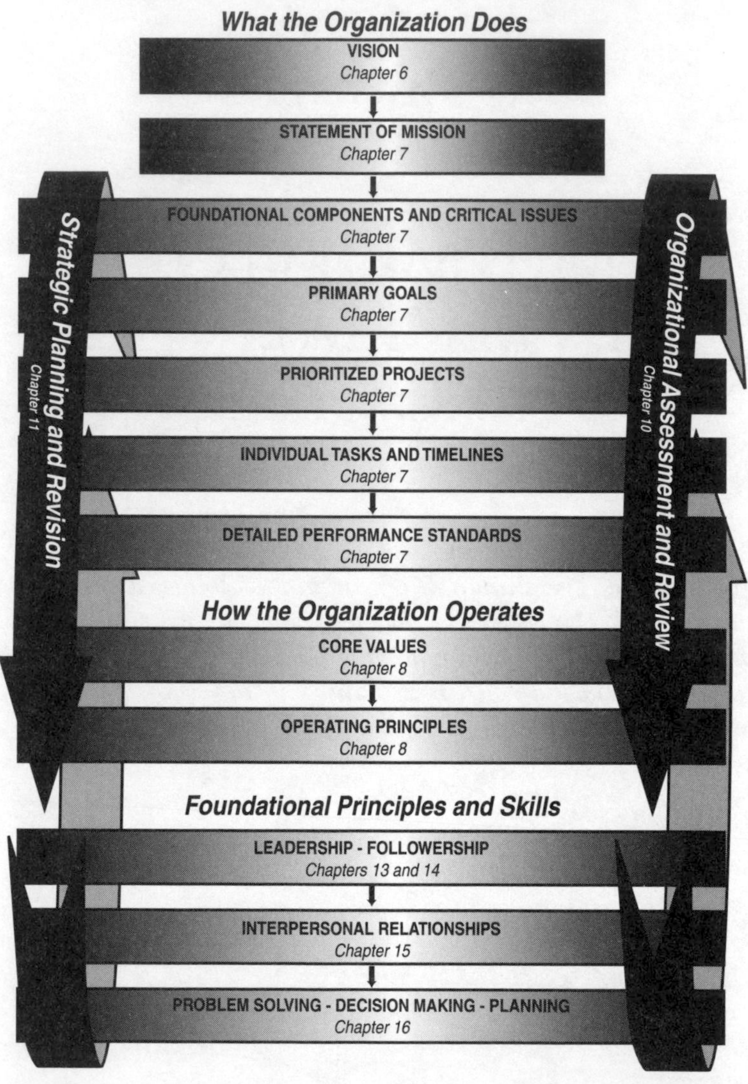

CHAPTER 6

A NEW VISION IS BORN

I was shocked by the expression on the young manager's face as he approached me at the end of a recent seminar. Tears on his cheeks were the outward expression of pain inside. Obviously, something I had said about relationships had brought his pent-up emotions to the surface. During our bittersweet conversation he told of all that he had learned about life in recent years. He slowly explained that his world had collapsed when his wife decided to leave him after eight years of marriage. A worn photograph from his wallet spoke volumes about their lives together. In it was my new friend, his wife, and their son and daughter. The children looked as if the Creator had used the same pattern for them as for their parents.

In the background were the family home, two new cars, and a newly constructed swimming pool. I complimented him on his beautiful family, and then, to try to cheer him, I mentioned his impressive house. His response proved that he really had learned a lot.

"The house is a monument to my stupidity!" he spewed. "I built it by working every hour of overtime I possibly could. I was never home. Even on Sundays, I worked a second job until late at night. At first, we were so happy there, but soon the excitement wore off. My wife asked me to cut back on some of the overtime. She said that we needed to make some changes, but I didn't listen. I just kept working . . . and now she is gone. Man, I never saw it coming."

My heart ached for this young man as he put his memories back into his wallet and headed for the door to leave. I pondered what he had shared with me. What had he done wrong? Was his big mistake too much overtime work? Not exactly. As I see it, the overtime was a symptom. The real problem was that he failed to recognize that it was time to change. This caused him to drive through his wife's verbal stop signs and ultimately crash. What is painfully obvious is that he had one vision for his family while his wife had another, conflicting vision. The result of their lack of agreement was all too predictable: division. Two visions in conflict. What was needed in that situation was extensive discussion between husband and wife about what they each wanted for their family. This type of dialogue could have changed a house divided into a house united.

The concept of vision has two elements. The first, *innovation*, involves a totally new idea for an organization, project, or undertaking. In the 1960s, American president John F. Kennedy had a new vision for the U.S. space program. He wanted to put a man on the moon. Since this had never been done, there was no existing plan to modify or change. It all had to be designed from the beginning.

The second element of vision involves *revision,* or improving on something that is already in existence. It is common for leaders of organizations to want to improve on their organization's current performance, just as professional athletes want to raise the level of their effectiveness. In an organizational setting, a new vision is conceived when leaders become aware of the need for change. This may sound too simple, but in my experience, many leaders are like my new friend from the seminar. They don't realize that their nations, businesses, or families are at risk and in desperate need of change. These people fly through life blinded by the pace or complexity of it all until something happens that makes them shift from autopilot to manual controls. Then they finally recognize the need for a serious mid-course adjustment for themselves and/or their organizations.

In the business arena, awareness of the need to change may come from a variety of positive experiences, such as reading books, attending conferences, or talking with others who are changing their own organizations. Unfortunately, awareness of the need to change often comes from extremely negative experiences as well. Employees go on strike, customers leave, spouses demand divorce, and children run away from home. Too often, the leaders involved are caught off guard by the crises that now confront them. I counsel many leaders who lament, "I never saw it coming." Nine times out of ten we never see a problem coming because we never take the time to look.

I counsel many leaders who lament, "I never saw it coming." Nine times out of ten we never see a problem coming because we never take the time to look.

A new vision is created in response to new conditions, which can be either positive or negative. Even during productive times, a leader may see a significant opportunity for growth, improvement, or advancement of the existing vision. Conversely, a leader may identify threatening circumstances, conditions, and trends that have the potential to destroy the organization. Either scenario should stimulate the creation of a new vision. Even during the best of times, it makes sense to pause and ponder your organization's past, present, and future. The discoveries can be amazing. Are your employees still smiling when they work? Does your spouse still like to talk with you about important matters? Are your product sales dropping? What innovations has your organization produced lately? Has your vision become cloudy, or is it still crystal clear? Leaders who invest ninety seconds each day reflecting on these questions should never be caught off guard again.

THREE CONDITIONS

People who take the time to investigate will discover that each aspect of their family, church, business, or government falls into one of three conditions or classifications. First is the *ideal* state, where no improvement is needed. This is a rare condition, but it can happen. In a family setting there are many areas that need to be checked. For example, the Smith family consists of a husband, wife, and three children. Every six months, they sit down and specifically talk about the family's relationships, finances, location, education, and health. During one discussion, they agree that the relationships are supportive, there are sufficient funds for the family's well-being, everyone is pleased with where they live, the school system is doing a great job of educating the children, and they are all in excellent health. The obvious response to these ideal elements is to leave them alone. Change for the sake of change is meddling.

The second possibility is that some areas are *acceptable with room for improvement*. With some fine tuning, these weaker parts can become exceptional components of the operation, propelling it towards it's mission. There will be many opportunities for improvement in technology, communications, productivity, quality, leadership, and relationships in every type of organization. To illustrate, let's say that the next time the Smith family meets for their "state-of-the-family" discussion, some things have changed. Mom and the oldest child don't seem as close as in the past. Mr. Smith's blood pressure is up slightly. The youngest child's grades at school are beginning to drop.

None of these conditions indicates a crisis, but they could indicate the start of a negative trend. Even though each situation is still acceptable, the family takes action now to move closer to the ideal condition that they have enjoyed in the past. Mom and the oldest child agree to spend some special time together to rebuild the bond between them. Dad begins to exercise and modify his diet to control his blood pressure. The older children agree to help the youngest with schoolwork until her grades return to normal. The family's timely analysis and commitment to excellence keep it functioning at near peak performance.

The third possibility is that some aspects are completely *unacceptable* and must be totally renewed. Again, we will use the Smith family as an example. During their next meeting, they discover the quality of their relationships is deteriorating at a frightening rate. Mr. Smith's health is failing. His company is about to downsize, which may cost him his job. The children's grades have dropped dramatically. Without a new vision, the Smith family will be destroyed.

Clearly, this is not a time for minor adjustments to the family. Significant improvements need to be made. A thorough analysis must be done to determine what caused the problems in the first place. This information is then used to radically redesign the family's approach to relationships and develop a plan for financial stability. From the chaos and confusion, a new vision for a better future of the Smith family is born.

THE VISION IS BORN

Remember that in the field of organizational development there are two basic types of visions: innovation and revision. Innovations are completely new ideas, entities, concepts, products, businesses, and so forth. The great inventions of history, like the wheel, electricity, and room service, were all innovations. Revisions occur when people analyze existing conditions or situations in their organizations and discover ways to improve them. While not many people actually invent something new during their lifetimes, we all have opportunities to make something better. Look at the word *revision.* Dissect it. *Re* means to return or revisit something. *Vision* is the original idea or concept. Combined, this word compels us to return to the original purpose of our business, ministry, family, or nation to determine whether we are still on course. It is never too late to *re-vise* any aspect of our personal or professional lives.

Once a person is convinced that a vision is worth pursuing, he should be prepared to sacrifice to see it fulfilled.

Once the leadership of any organization has identified opportunities for improvement or serious threats to its existence, it is time to clarify and communicate the new vision to others who can help birth the changes. The vision should be far-reaching and broad in scope. It should stimulate people's imaginations with new possibilities for themselves, their nations, businesses, or families. It is time to dream the greatest dream imaginable. People today are looking for hope and a challenge. We need something larger than our own interests to pursue. We need a large enough vision to pull us away from the countless distractions that steal our energy and lull us into complacency—something of greater significance than television, computers, sports, and the pursuit of greater personal wealth. We need visions that break the power of apathy and the spirit of defeatism.

Is this possible? Without question it is! Families are developing new visions for close relationships. In drug-ravaged inner cities, individuals with vision are buying and repairing groups of abandoned houses. These homes are then sold to families interested in building productive, crime-free neighborhoods. New businesses are started each day as people with vision discover innovative products and services they can market. Political leaders are beginning to govern by principles of integrity, fairness, and concern for the well-being of their people. Positive change can happen. Positive change will happen. It only takes a new vision!

EXPECTED RESULTS

The fire of change is fueled by positive expectations. Leaders are motivated by the realization that positive change produces a less stressful environment, improved trust, greater commitment from followers, and improved bottom-line performance. A slightly less tangible result of a new vision is the tremendous amount of satisfaction that leaders receive as they see growth in their organizations, their followers, and themselves. Initiating and managing change takes a great deal of hard work and occasionally can seem overwhelming. During these times of emotional challenge, it helps to reflect on the brighter future that awaits those who persevere beyond today's pressures.

COMMITMENT

As any parent can attest, the process of conception is much different than the labor of delivery. Labor and delivery take much more time and patience and, unfortunately, produce a great deal of pain. So it is with change initiatives. We can be certain that once a new vision has been conceived, much labor will follow.

This is where the virtue of commitment is applied. Once a person is convinced that a vision is worth pursuing, he should be prepared to sacrifice to see it fulfilled. When we were expecting Steven, our second child, my wife experienced complications during the pregnancy. Premature labor forced her to remain strictly in bed for almost six months to ensure that the baby would have time to develop. She had sporadic contractions during the entire six months. No less than five times she was rushed to the hospital. Each time, we were in danger of losing our unborn son. Through it all, she maintained the vision of a healthy child who would be born if she could endure the difficulty of the pregnancy and the pain of delivery. My wife demonstrated the qualities necessary to see a vision through to birth. She showed a tremendous amount of courage, determination, and patience. She was faithful to the end, and by the grace of God, our son was born in perfect health. There is no substitute for commitment, and there is nothing to commit to without a vision.

QUESTIONS AND REFLECTIONS

Business • Government • Ministry • Family • Personal

1. When did you last evaluate your organization's vision? Are there elements that need to be changed?

2. What parts of your organization are in ideal condition?

3. What parts of your organization are acceptable with room for improvement?

4. What parts of your organization are unacceptable and need to be changed?

CHAPTER 7

CLEAR PURPOSE AND DIRECTION

As human beings, our souls cry out for purpose. We are restless and lack peace until our lives have real meaning. Without solid direction, we are like children lost in a crowd, unsure of our next move.

So it is with organizations. This same collective cry for direction and relevance is barely audible above the din of the day's distractions, but it is there nonetheless. Our families, churches, businesses, and nations are perishing from lack of clear direction. Organizational leaders must understand fully where they are going and how they will get there if they hope to be productive. Imagine the chaos if two teams involved in a sporting event were playing by different sets of rules. What would happen in a marriage if the husband and wife failed to agree on the basic foundations for their relationship? There would be constant problems and arguments. These examples may seem absurd, and yet countless organizations try to operate without clarifying what they are trying to achieve or how they will achieve it.

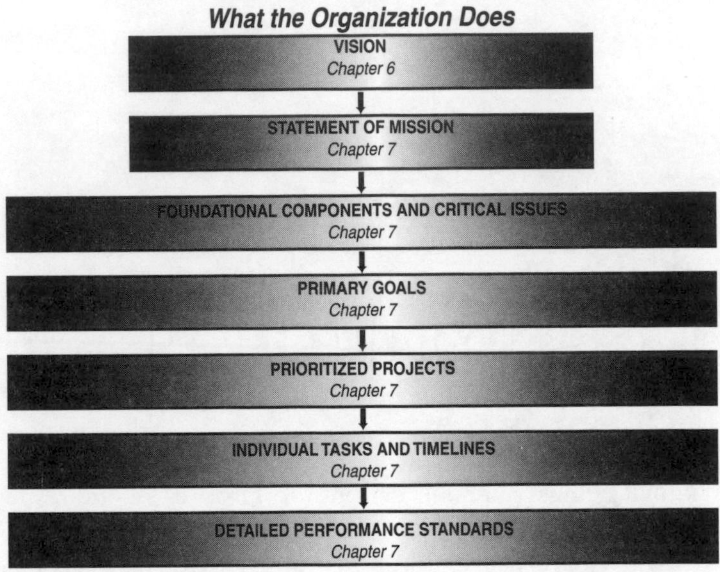

In the business world, the lack of attention to these issues causes tremendous problems with employees, customers, and suppliers. At the national level, this results in citizen apathy and mistrust of leaders whose positions on important issues sway like reeds in the wind. In chapter 6, we addressed the need for leaders to establish a new vision—something to reach for. The next step: to be effective, each organization must bring its vision down to earth and clarify how it will accomplish its vision. This is achieved by writing a specific statement of mission for the organization. The importance of this step cannot be overstated. Too often, we assume that our employees understand their roles, responsibilities, and how their performances contribute to the organization's ultimate success. In many instances, this is simply not true. Countless employees don't understand what is expected of them on a daily basis. They may comprehend their basic duties, but are unclear about the fine details of their work. Further, they are often unsure of how their performances impact their coworkers in other departments, areas, units, or divisions.

I recently spoke with the president of a large banking institution about the value of clear purpose and direction. He had asked for advice on how to unify his sizable workforce. One of my initial questions to him dealt with his vision and statement of mission. His response was fascinating. He casually said that their mission statement had been created several years earlier and was "just fine." Before I could ask what "just fine" meant, he added that none of his employees had seen or heard about the statement for the past two years. Just fine?

For best performance, all employees must understand what is expected of them and how the work of the entire organization is linked. This understanding begins when employees are well versed in the organization's written statement of mission. The following statement of mission guides the operation of my consulting and training company. *The associates of Molitor International will demonstrate and teach foundational principles of leadership, teamwork, and problem solving to business, government, religious, and family organizations to assist them in the achievement of their respective missions.*

Because our work focuses heavily on interpersonal relationships, we were able to include both the typical directional components and a cultural component in our statement of mission. The directional components of our statement clarify who we intend to work with—business, governments, and so forth—and also, what we intend to impart—leadership, teamwork, and so forth—to those clients. The cultural aspect of the statement is captured in the word *demonstrate*. In chapter 8, we will expand on the cultural component for all types of organizations.

In our statement of mission, the word *demonstrate* is underlined for one simple reason: It is understood that if our associates are unable to demonstrate these foundational principles, they are not ready to teach them to other people. This understanding is pivotal to our continued success as an organization.

Unlike some mission statements that end up as dust collectors on office walls, we actually use ours. For example, when we interview potential employees, we spend time discussing this statement in detail to confirm what it means. It must be clear to prospective employees that we provide specialized services and operate according to a specific code of conduct. This practice has benefited our company and prospective employees as well. For example, interviewees who are not interested in being part of an organization that strives to maintain high standards of conduct often eliminate themselves from consideration after the initial meeting. This saves everyone a great deal of time, money, and frustration. Also, people who are aligned with these standards adjust quickly to our empowered work environment. Our employees are able to use our statement of mission and core values to make autonomous work-related decisions. This frees our leaders to spend time on our own mission rather than cleaning up messes caused by misguided or unprincipled employees.

New businesses rarely struggle with whether writing down their mission statement, core values, and operating principles is important. However, this process often seems unnecessary to those in charge of existing organizations. Why? Because they are already doing *something* that occupies their time. Obviously, restaurants are currently preparing and serving food, hospitals are taking care of the sick, and businesses are making products. Assuming that each of the enterprises is currently profitable, does it still make sense for them to write down the obvious? Definitely! What is obvious to some members of the organizations is anything but obvious to others. Profits, performance, and commitment can be increased when everyone is clear on the proper direction and priorities.

The restaurant owner is very clear about her vision for excellent service, so why do some customers dine once and never return? Her newly hired servers are unaware of her vision and often treat customers with indifference. The hospital with excellent leadership continues to receive excessive complaints from patients. The reason? Many staff members have not personalized the leaders' passion for service, so patients receive inconsistent care.

To be effective, each organization must bring its vision down to earth and clarify how it will accomplish its vision.

Leaders who hope to remain competitive should take the time to write a clear statement of mission and communicate it to everyone impacted by it. During the communication process, the mission statement must be interpreted and personalized so that everyone's performance is linked and aligned with the mission. The written statement is the means to the end, not the end itself. That is, it is not sufficient just to write these things on a sheet of paper. Employees in many businesses don't have a clue why management ever bothered to write down the company mission statement. Too often, employees view the mission statement as a meaningless document that top management wasted two weeks in a posh resort creating, without ever knowing what they would do with it when it was completed. However, management's credibility and the company's viability skyrocket once the mission statement becomes the guiding light for *all* employee activities.

THE BIG PICTURE

Over the years, I have learned that people often are confused by terms such as *vision, mission, values, goals,* and *objectives.* This is not because the words are difficult to comprehend, but because they may be used interchangeably. One company calls their overall statement of purpose a *vision* statement. Another calls theirs a *mission* statement, and so on. Fortunately, it does not matter what terms are used as long as everyone in the organization understands what they mean. Although it sounds like corporate blasphemy, I believe that the real value is not found in the vision or mission statement itself. Confirming my belief, throughout the world there are thousands of important mission statements gathering dust on office walls. The ultimate value of an organization's statement of purpose is to ensure that each and every task performed is linked to and aligned with the organization's overall vision.

It is crucial that organizations understand how their directional components work together to ensure proper focus of efforts and resources.

The following are seven basic components of an organization that describe and determine *what* the organization does. In descending order, they are:

1. Vision
2. Statement of mission
3. Foundational components and critical issues
4. Primary goals
5. Prioritized projects
6. Individual tasks and timelines
7. Detailed performance standards

Each component is linked to and aligned with those above it and provides additional details about the previous component as well. The following example should help to explain how the items are connected.

VISION

The vision is extremely broad, lofty, and intentionally uncluttered by details. Example: *I have a vision to see Molitor In-*

ternational become the most effective consulting and training firm in the world. This concept is easy to understand and definitely lofty, but it gives no real direction to any of my employees. Also, while it says something about *what* will be done, it says nothing about *how* it will be done. Its purpose simply is to focus attention on the ultimate reason for the organization to exist. [This vision represents a dream of mine that was birthed in the early 1980s.] I consider a vision as the starting point for discussion on what an organization is destined to do or become.

STATEMENT OF MISSION

The statement of mission adds detail to the vision and must be written. Consider this: *The associates of Molitor International will* demonstrate *and teach foundational principles of leadership, teamwork, and problem solving to business, government, religious, and family organizations to assist them in the achievement of their respective missions.*

This gives a clearer picture of what our organization seeks to do or become. It identifies the primary products and/or areas of service, and also the types of organizations that will be served. The statement of mission becomes the umbrella for every activity that takes place below it. No project or task should be undertaken that is not directly or ultimately linked to the statement of mission.

FOUNDATIONAL COMPONENTS AND CRITICAL ISSUES

Foundational components (FCs) are the most vital areas for an organization's success. They are the basic building blocks of the organization's mission. Asking two simple questions can identify foundational components. Why does our organization exist, and what are the basics that it requires to function? In manufacturing, FCs may include the type of product that the company produces, raw materials used in the manufacturing process, the company's infrastructure, machinery, information systems, human resources, the management team, and sales and marketing plan. Without these elements in place and functioning properly, the manufacturing organization will cease to exist as a viable company. For a hospital, some foundational components are its buildings, medical equipment, supplies, physicians, patients, hospital staff, communication systems, and information systems. If you took away any of these components, the hospital could not function.

In other words, foundational components are the essential elements that an organization must have in place for it to achieve its mission, and leaders must keep constant watch over the relative health of these vital areas.

FCs are not only physical things such as machinery and staff, but also involve functions, operations, outputs, and processes. Some examples include quality, productivity, profitability, marketing, and investment strategies. Each organization will have standard approaches and expectations for performance in these areas. As long as the performance remains at an acceptable or standard range, the organization continues to function properly.

This brings us to the subject of critical issues (CIs). These are conditions, issues, and problems that develop and could threaten the well-being of an organization. Critical issues may also come in the form of new opportunities that arise with the potential of improving the organization's profitability, productivity, quality, employee satisfaction, or other bottom line categories. Critical issues change—or at least should change—the priorities within an organization by forcing leaders to react to the new conditions.

Sadly, leaders sometimes fail to look for and identify the critical issues facing their organizations. They are too busy, too distracted, or too convinced that their current course of action is correct to consider reprioritizing the investment of their human, financial, or other resources. Often this lack of responsiveness to changing conditions does irreparable harm to the organization. Other leaders seem to acknowledge that new critical issues exist but still fail to properly reprioritize their efforts to deal with the new problems or opportunities.

Their problem with priority issues comes from a very basic human tendency to do first what we like to do and leave less enjoyable things for later. Also, we tend to focus our attention on activities at which we are most skilled, thereby leaving the tougher tasks undone, regardless of their relative priority to our organizational or personal success. In other words, we tend to major on minors and pass over critical tasks in favor of something more comfortable, rewarding, stimulating, or just plain fun.

We need to clarify and reevaluate our organization's CIs regularly. For example, at the start of a year a manufacturing organization's leaders may decide that one of their most critical issues is business expansion. They plan, allocate resources, and pursue new markets. However, midway through the year they are faced with new government regulations that require a complete product redesign. Failure to comply would be disastrous for the organization, so now what? The leaders need to add the product redesign to their list of CIs and determine whether they have sufficient resources to achieve the change, and still deal with other critical issues the organization is wrestling with. Let's say there is not enough manpower or finances to do everything this year. The next step is to compare the new critical issue of compliance with government regulations to preexisting projects. Is the product redesign a higher priority than ongoing research and development? Is it more important than servicing existing clients? Is it a higher priority than the planned expansion? The leaders would use their best judgment in reestablishing priorities of the CIs and expend their precious time, financial, and human resources on those that are the highest priority. Failure to do so is costly.

What happens when church leaders fail to identify and pursue their most critical issues in the proper priority? They conduct yet another conference for their congregation rather than venture into their community to minister to hurting lives. What is lost when warm Saturday afternoons entice fathers to spend their energies at the golf course rather than at home building solid relationships with their young children? Golf scores improve; families suffer.

An important by-product that comes from analyzing CIs is the identification of areas no longer relevant for an organization. For example, less than twelve months ago my staff and I concluded that we no longer fit in our corporate headquarters. Obviously, one of the most critical issues at that time was finding a new home for our company. We committed the funds, time, and personnel necessary to acquire the right building. Once we found our new building, this issue was no longer critical or even valid, and we reassigned our personnel to other priority duties. This transition was easy because of our relatively small size, limited levels of management, and open communication practices. However, in larger organizations, it is amazing how much time, money, and manpower are wasted pursuing issues that are not the most critical for success or are no longer valid. We need to check and recheck our organization's critical issues and priorities regularly. Once we have identified our current critical issues, then it is time to develop specific goals for each one.

PRIMARY GOALS

Primary goals are used to clarify further what must be done to accomplish the mission. Remember, at this stage the mission has been subdivided into minimissions, or foundational components. Leaders constantly watch for critical issues, new problems, and opportunities that arise. Each foundational component or critical issue is analyzed, prioritized, and further divided into primary goals. Some organizations may refer to these as objectives. Whatever they are called, these goals must be written and clear to everyone who is impacted by them.

All too often, each division of an organization—department, function, unit, plant, and so forth—concentrates on its own fairly broad goals and is not aware of or concerned with the goals of other divisions. This is a huge mistake! I believe that primary goals should be communicated across all departments, units, and divisions as a means of coordinating the organization's overall effort.

Also, goals are often pursued without regard to or without a real understanding of the mission. This is a form of organizational suicide. I have found that for peak organizational performance, all goals must be linked directly to the mission statement and clearly communicated to every other part of the organization. Then, as each department achieves its respective goals, the foundational components will be optimized and the mission will be accomplished.

Primary goals identify specific targets and measurements for each foundational component and/or critical issue. For example, one of the foundational components of my business deals with our individual leadership coaching process, called EXECUTIVE *A PLUS*. This involves a detailed process of gathering 360-degree feedback from a person's peers, leaders, and followers to enhance this person's leadership performance.

At a recent staff meeting, we discovered that we had too much variation in the number of responses we get to the leadership surveys that are sent out. Also, we had excessive variation in the length of time that our coaches spend with each candidate. Some take sixteen weeks, while others take up to twenty weeks. Since the EXECUTIVE *A PLUS* process is a foundational component of our business, we set goals for improvement. We determined that there were three primary goals to make the process more efficient and cost effective, while maintaining the positive impact on our clients. Our first goal was to increase the number of survey responses to at least 80 percent returned. Second, we wanted to standardize the length of time spent with each person being coached. Our research showed that sixteen weeks was the optimal duration for the EXECUTIVE *A PLUS* process.

Third, we wanted to redesign the format so that survey results were returned to the candidate in a more logical sequence.

Once we established these primary goals, we assigned each goal to members of our staff. It then became each staff person's responsibility to determine how to accomplish the goal. The first step is for them to view the goal as a series of projects to be organized and prioritized.

PRIORITIZED PROJECTS

At this stage, things get very exciting as all of our previous planning is translated into specific actions. Our mission points the way, and our foundational components focus attention on what really counts. We have created primary goals, with measurements and timelines for each FC and CI that must be addressed. Then, each goal has been assigned to an individual who subdivides it into a series of projects in order of priority. This organized approach ensures that nothing is left to chance and that all efforts are moving toward the mission.

For example, the goal of obtaining more responses to our EXECUTIVE *A PLUS* surveys is assigned to Shaenon, our office manager. To achieve this goal, she divides it into three projects. First, she decides to research our database to collect information on the actual amount of variation we have in the process. Second, Shaenon decides to interview a cross section of previous

EXECUTIVE *A PLUS* candidates for their views on how to increase the response rates. Third, she studies our current survey forms to determine if they can be simplified for faster completion. She is confident that when these projects are complete, they will accomplish our primary goal of increased responses to the EXECUTIVE *A PLUS* surveys. Now that she has subdivided the primary goal into manageable projects, Shaenon enlists other staff members to help complete them. An essential part of her discussion with them is the clarification of individual tasks and timelines. This attention to detail will maximize the effectiveness and timeliness of each project.

INDIVIDUAL TASKS AND TIMELINES

This final directional component deals with individual tasks that are undertaken daily by each member of the organization. Making phone calls, entering data into computers, and attending meetings are individual tasks that combine to complete broader projects. Each person should understand how his daily tasks help the organization achieve its ultimate mission. Many years ago, a creative songwriter came up with a catchy tune that detailed how our bones are all connected to one another. Countless people bounced through their days singing, "The thigh bone's connected to the knee bone, the knee bone's connected to the leg bone, the leg bone's connected to the foot bone," and so on. This lively song's message reflected how our lives are connected to those around us. However, I always think of that tune when teaching about purpose and direction. It is too easy to forget that what each person does in an organization is somehow linked to what others do.

Perhaps some new songwriter can put this to music. "The task is connected to the project, the project's connected to the goal, the goal is connected to the FC, the FC is connected to the mission, and the mission is connected to the vision." Our new song may not become a number one hit, but it certainly will help organizations remember how to be effective.

It is important to remember that each task must also include a timeline. *When* a task is to be performed is often as important as the task itself. This linked and aligned approach inspires proper focus and highlights that each person's contribution is extremely valuable to the organization.

DETAILED PERFORMANCE STANDARDS

For every task that is performed in an organization, there is both a proper time and a preferred way to perform it. Leaders should determine which tasks are critical to the success of the operation, and communicate so that everyone involved understands exactly how to complete the tasks. The expectations related to who, what, where, when, and how each task is to be completed must be clear. Some of these tasks will need to have written instructions called detailed performance standards (DPS) to ensure that there is no misunderstanding or variation in their accomplishment. Leaders must review and update performance standards regularly to maintain peak performance. At Molitor International we have written detailed performance standards for such things as travel policies, billing procedures, phone answering protocol, and addressing client concerns. The small investment of time required to compile this information has been repaid many times over in the form of smoother operations.

For every task that is performed in an organization, there is a proper way to perform it.

This chapter has covered the purpose and directional issues. In essence, this is *what* an organization does and the way to ensure that each person's activities are linked and aligned with those around them. Next, we must clarify how an organization operates by identifying its core values and operating principles.

QUESTIONS AND REFLECTIONS

Business • Government • Ministry • Family • Personal

1. What is the mission of your organization? Do all members of the organization understand your mission?

2. What are your organization's foundational components? Why does it exist?

3. What are the most critical issues facing your organization today?

4. Are the activities of all members of your organization linked and aligned?

5. Does your organization have written detailed performance standards for everyone's activities?

THE MOLITOR DEVELOPMENTAL PROCESS

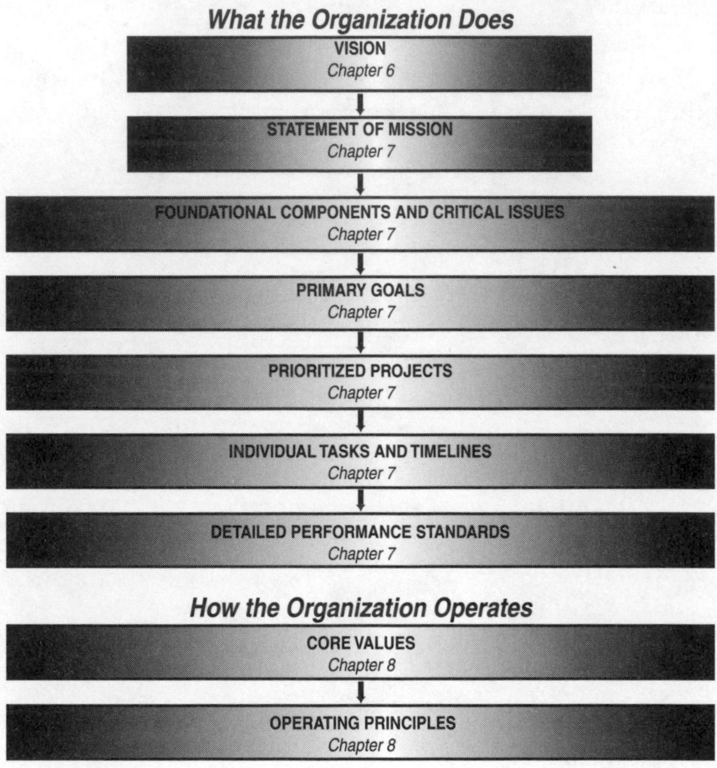

Chapter 8

CORE VALUES AND OPERATING PRINCIPLES

"I've got it," yelled the agitated worker. "I'll hide in the parking lot after work, and when the boss comes out to his car, I'll shoot him in the arm. You know—just a flesh wound. Then maybe he'll listen when we try to talk to him!"

No, this is not a line from a gangster movie. It is an actual proposal from a group of employees discussing a communication problem they were having with their supervisor. I was trying to help this group design a strategy for improved labor-management relationships when this bizarre suggestion surfaced. This was one frustrated employee's best suggestion on how to deal with his supervisor. The scariest part of the idea is that the rest of the group was ready to approve the plan. Tough bunch! I quickly began an unplanned teaching on core values that changed their minds. The concept of core values saved the supervisor's skin—and possibly his life—if the employee's aim was as bad as his suggestion.

CORE VALUES ARE NOT RULES AND REGULATIONS

In an organizational setting, core values are those beliefs that are held in the highest esteem. They are the principles and standards upon which the organization intends to build its future. Core values such as honesty, fairness, and respect for all individuals shape the behavior of every person involved with the organization.

Core values are different from an organization's list of rules or employment policies. A company often has an employee handbook, which outlines a wide variety of regulations—do's and don'ts that every person is supposed to adhere to. The problem with most handbooks is that in their attempt to clarify how each and every situation is to be handled, they become incredibly cumbersome. This creates a situation in which most employees don't even bother trying to learn all of the policies because there are too many. Those employees who do learn all of them often do so in an attempt to discover loopholes and ways to "beat the system." Excessive rules and regulations are paralyzing to first-line supervisors who quickly learn that they risk the wrath of the rule book if they make logical work-related decisions about employee conduct, customer complaints, or other subjects.

The other problem with complicated rule books is that they tend to eliminate synergistic discussions among employees and managers alike. When a situation arises that needs resolution, it can be very powerful to have people check the decision against the core values and then brainstorm a unique solution.

I predict that the problems and challenges that will face leaders in the near future will require much more than a simple interpretation of rules by a corporate referee. To remain competitive, we must solve problems in the framework of our company values rather than on the basis of some rule that was written for a former generation of managers.

HOW THE ORGANIZATION OPERATES

In chapter 7, we examined the various issues that provide direction for the organization. These directional components include vision, mission, foundational components and critical issues, primary goals, prioritized projects, and individual tasks. These serve to clarify why the organization exists and what goods and/or services the organization provides. They further define the roles and responsibilities of each member of the organization so it can produce its goods and services can be produced in a highly efficient manner. In essence, the directional components clarify *what* the organization does. This is a good beginning; however, for peak performance, we also must clarify one additional foundation of the organization: its culture. The following cultural components of core values and operating principles clarify *how* people are to interact with others, both inside and outside of the organization.

CORE VALUES

Vision and mission deal primarily with what an organization does, not how it intends to operate. Therefore, to understand the organization more completely, we must know its core values. These stated standards, by which members of the organization agree to live at work, explain the origin and nature of the organization's collective character. Core values may be recorded in a list of individual ideals or placed in an all-encompassing statement. For example, I use the following statement to highlight my company's core values: *We will strive to be known by our customers, suppliers, coworkers, and others in the world community as people of fairness, integrity, honesty, caring, respect, and diligence.* As this statement shows, core values establish an organization's general attitude and approach to business ethics and morality.

CULTURE BY DESIGN OR DEFAULT?

Amazingly, many leaders attempt to operate their businesses, ministries, governments, or families without ever clarifying what type of culture they desire. Whenever this happens, they invariably end up with a culture by default rather than by design. It is safe to say that whenever any organization is allowed to develop without the benefit of guiding values and principles, it quickly will fragment into multiple subcultures. In this disintegrated state, each member of the organization establishes personal standards of acceptable behavior toward coworkers and customers. Throughout the world, many organizations operate in a state of controlled chaos as their members set standards of conduct and performance that fit their personal paradigms. The negative impact of these diverse standards is profound. Adversarial labor-management relations, sexual harassment, workplace dishonesty, and low customer satisfaction often find their roots in the soil of unclear core values.

Core values reveal the heart and character of an organization as quickly as they reveal the heart and character of a person. Consider the introductions that take place at a party or similar event. Have you ever met this person?

"Hello, I'm Mr. Smith, and I'm the president of the XYZ Company."

Normally, people are swift to reveal their names and what they do, but not much about who they are. Shortly after the introduction, Joe will slip some status statements into the conversation. That he lives in the ritzy section of town, drives an expensive car, has just returned from a fabulous vacation, and is about to finalize a big business deal have an amazing way of being revealed early in the discussion. Perhaps this is one reason that many of us avoid this type of gathering. We know that we won't take the time to get past the superficial at a party, so why bother? Experience has proven that what someone does or what they have reveals little about who they really are as a person.

Would you enter into a partnership with Mr. Smith after this introduction? After all, he is obviously successful. If your answer is no, I applaud you. Too much is at stake to base your trust on external indicators. All too often marriages, alliances, and partnerships have dissolved because they were established on superficial rather than relevant issues. Even Adolph Hitler's stated vision for his country sounded good. It included national pride, high levels of employment, and prosperity. At first glance, it would be difficult for anyone to find fault with what he proposed. This is why it is crucial that Hitler's core values are seen along with his mission. The picture becomes clear when we see *how* he wanted to accomplish his dream. History reveals that his core values included hatred, prejudice, lust for power, violence, and, ultimately, genocide. We must remember that core values and mission are inseparable. The mission is the desired end and the core values are a primary means to that end.

What someone does or what they have says little about who they really are.

Since these foundational standards determine an organization's culture, they are just as important as the vision and mission. I once had the opportunity to help a pastor analyze the lack of unity among the members of his staff. They all truly wanted the church to grow and seemed to have a great deal in common. Also, they were all sincere in their faith and clearly agreed on the mission of the church. We eventually discovered that the problem involved conflicting core values among the leaders. Some leaders believed that the church should be run according to a long list of rules and regulations. Any violation meant expulsion from membership. Other leaders believed that some rules were appropriate, but there should be ample room for mercy, grace, and tolerance. Once this difference was uncovered and clarified, the leaders were able to work together to forge a new understanding of the church's core values. Their final agreement was found between the two original positions. Several leaders were unable to commit to the revised list of core values and resigned. This was far better than the alternative of extended infighting, confusion, and, ultimately, a split congregation.

In my own organization, I make sure that we have a common understanding of such concepts as dedication to clients, caring for others, and respect for one another. These core values form the foundation for the moral and ethical codes that enable our organization to prosper. While I do not believe that morality can be legislated, I am certain that standards of moral behavior are both possible and necessary. Morality is an internal issue that comes from what is in our hearts—only God can change that. But moral behavior comes when we have clear definitions of what is acceptable in an organization—core values—and we receive appropriate rewards or consequences for our actions. In my experience, people raise or lower their behavior to the accepted standards. Therefore, when I hire new associates I make sure they understand that they are expected to commit to our company's core values of honesty, integrity, caring for others, respect for one another, personal responsibility, and excellence in work performed.

I realize that some people may struggle with the concepts of core values. Core values may be perceived as being too negative, too controlling, or as an enemy of *diversity,* one of the buzzwords of 1990s. Let me be very clear about the current application of diversity in the workplace: I value individual freedom more than life itself. I have no use for hard-hearted, prejudiced, oppressive governments, managers, religious leaders, or leaders like this of any kind, for that matter. If diversity means working with people from different backgrounds, races, genders, or ages, then I strongly support diversity. Further, I am convinced that this type of diversity, when coupled with clearly defined core values, creates a highly desirable, dynamic environment in any organization.

However, I am equally convinced that the following is true: Freedom without rules, laws, and boundaries soon becomes anarchy. Diversity without standards quickly degrades into perversity—anything in word or deed becomes acceptable. Is this an exaggeration of the potential problem? Hardly. In recent history, groups have exercised their diverse religious freedoms by committing mass suicide, leaving a multitude of grieving family members behind.

Also, consider an example from the next frontier of the new millennium: cyberspace. The Internet has made the teachings, products, services, and personal messages of a growing number of people available to the entire world. Innovative global businesses are formed, long-distance commerce is conducted, new friendships are created, and children learn about the mysteries of science on the Internet. This technological wonder has produced countless other benefits as well. While the Internet gets an incredibly high grade in its mission of worldwide information exchange, it fails miserably in the area of core values. Let me explain.

In the late 1990s there were few established standards for what could and could not be transmitted on the Internet. The result? Predictably, people with core values that differ from the norm began to push the decency envelope. Some tried to use computer networks to steal trade secrets and money from other companies. Others used it as an outlet to make a wide range of hard-core pornographic materials accessible to people of all ages. The degeneration continued as pedophiles used the Internet to contact young, innocent victims. Naturally, many solid citizens became alarmed and spoke against unrestricted use of such a powerful system. Just as naturally, people who opposed any restrictions on what they perceived to be their rights and freedoms rose up to defend these diverse uses of the Internet. The battle was on; and due to the Internet's international reach, it will continue for many years. Some forms of diversity are definitely not good, and any organization that fails to clarify its own core values eventually will have to deal with diversity-gone-wild.

To summarize, the Internet itself is neither good nor bad; it is just a tool or vehicle for information transfer. Governments, communication experts, and international lawyers eventually will agree on a set of standards to protect network users and still allow individual freedom. When they are finished, the result will be a list of core values, although they may call it something entirely different.

Whether we are dealing with communication networks or grocery stores, the ideal situation encourages people to express themselves freely in widely diverse ways within the boundaries of clearly defined standards. That is why it is vital that the leaders of every organization clarify their core values when they convey their mission. Then the mission is truly the destination, and the core values represent the method used to get there.

MOVING FROM THEORY TO REALITY

It is the leaders of an organization who should develop the list of core values. It is not a joint project in which every employee gets a vote or where a simple majority decides what the core values should be. To be genuine, the organization's values must reflect the values of its leaders. There are many valid opportunities for follower involvement within an organization. However, the creation of its foundational standards is definitely not one of them. If you involve people in the wrong decisions, you surely will suffer for having done so.

I recall hearing about an incident that happened on a college campus during the rebellious 1960s. To generate some excitement for the student body, the administration decided to change the official school colors and select a new mascot for its athletic program. Historically, school officials would make these decisions without involving students. The officials would select a rich combination of colors, perhaps a striking blend of red and blue or black and gold. Then, in order to complete the transformation, the officials would choose a powerful animal, such a lion, bear, or falcon, for the mascot. However, during these nontraditional days, the school officials wanted to try something different by involving the students in the decision-making process.

The idea didn't work as planned. Like doting grandfathers, they agreed to let students vote to determine the new school colors and mascot. Unfortunately, the students, who at that time were focused on other matters like the war in Vietnam and the military draft, made a mockery of what they considered trivial matters. They carefully orchestrated a plan to send a message to school officials. If my memory serves me correctly, the school colors selected by the students were hot pink and florescent orange. Also, they selected an artichoke as the new school mascot. I pity the poor person who had to rewrite the school's song. Whoever heard of the Fighting Artichokes? Obviously, school officials had to invalidate the selections and returned to their original colors and mascot.

The school leaders were not wrong in trying somehow to involve students in the decision-making process. However, in this instance the leaders' approach was more one of abdication than involvement. School colors and mascots play a significant role in defining the image of a school. They are building blocks in the culture of a school, just as core values shape the culture of other organizations. While it is wise to ask for involvement and suggestions from others, I am convinced that leaders must make decisions regarding an organization's core values.

I have worked with leaders of many companies to clarify their core values, and then to develop strategies for communicating the core values to the workforce. This second step, communication with the workforce, is essential for establishing or reestablishing an organization's culture. I recently had the pleasure of working on this process with a team of employees from a large health care organization. Our plan was to design and facilitate a comprehensive cultural orientation process for the organization's three thousand-plus employees. After weeks of planning, we created a series of four-hour orientation sessions that included speeches from company officers, fact-filled handouts and brochures, motivating videotape presentations, and a time for questions and answers. The session design even included hundreds of door prizes of shirts, hats, and gift certificates for attendees.

To accommodate the massive number of employees and allow them to attend during work hours, we had to create a schedule that extended over several weeks. We designed the program content with one primary goal in mind: to provide each employee with a complete understanding of the organization's cultural and directional components. Therefore, we covered the organization's vision, mission, and core values and specifically how each employee could help to promote these foundational elements. We spent a significant amount of time talking about the behavioral expectations for each employee and that leaders would operate according to a set of foundational principles as they pursued organizational excellence. At the end of each session, we presented a long-term plan for training and development that would involve each member of the organization. The plan included team building, leadership development, mentoring, and other initiatives designed to help leaders and followers alike operate according to the expectations.

The financial investment for the cultural orientation was significant, with direct costs exceeding fifty thousand dollars. In addition, the organization paid all the expenses, which included the cost of the meeting hall, food and refreshments for the employees, handout materials, and door prizes. Because the meetings took place during work hours, the organization paid employees for attending, which cost approximately two hundred thousand dollars. When the final meeting ended, the sheer magnitude of the task had exhausted everyone involved.

We naturally asked ourselves the question that every leader should ask after making such an investment: Was the initiative successful? The answer to this question is a conditional yes. Yes, the meetings were well designed and facilitated. Yes, the speakers were convincing. Yes, the employees loved the door prizes and were excited about the plan for training and development. Finally, yes, everyone who attended left with a clear understanding of behavioral expectations, and therefore understood the desired corporate culture. However, the long-term answer can be given only when there is adequate follow-up, support, and accountability for the desired behaviors. If a few rogue managers are allowed to abuse employees in the future, it will not take long for the culture to disintegrate. If a few lazy employees are allowed to shirk critical duties related to patient care, the culture will begin to devolve into something less than what was desired. Even with this degree of uncertainty, it was well worth the effort. Had we not informed the workforce of the cultural expectations, I can guarantee that the organization would never reach its potential.

CORE VALUES AND ALLIANCES

Core values are also used to make decisions about alliances, partnerships, and relationships with people outside the organization.

It is vital to understand that an organization's success often attracts people and other organizations that may not share the same core values. They may come offering their services, assistance, resources, and finances. They may insist that they are totally compatible because they offer a similar service or product. Similarities like this are good starting points for discussion, but they are not nearly enough to form the basis of an alliance or coalition.

A friend of mine, John, owns a small company that developed an innovative computer product in the early 1990s. After years of hard work, he perfected the product and received a patent for it. From the beginning, he established core values of integrity, honesty, and fairness in all business dealings. His success brought attention from some of the largest firms in the world that use this type of product. He was "wined and dined" numerous times by representatives of these companies as each sought to become a partner with or buy into John's company. They spoke in glowing terms about the virtues of their respective companies.

Each day, millions of people stand on their core values in government, business, church, and family situations.

However, some interesting things happened when they had further meetings to discuss possible business relationships. The wining turned sour as some representatives now began to complain to John about their own company's poor cash flow and questioned the long-term value of John's product. More than once they were caught lying about the condition of the proposed alliance. Even with these drawbacks, they were prepared to offer huge sums of money to get a part of John's business. While the money was tempting, it was not difficult for John to make a decision. Clearly, his core values and those of the other companies were in direct conflict. A partnership with them would have been like putting an ox and a goat in the same harness. They would not have been able to work effectively together. John refused to form an alliance with these companies because of the difference in core values. Following his decision, his company tripled its financial worth and continues to prosper using his original core values.

An old cliché says, "Everyone has a price." In other words, for enough money, power, or other incentives, each person will forsake his basic values. I strongly reject that notion. I believe that each day millions of people stand on their core values in government, business, church, and family situations. This is a tribute to their character and proves the commitment to their respective missions.

OPERATING PRINCIPLES

Core values must be expanded and translated into operating principles—a code of conduct—for maximum effectiveness. This code must be communicated to each member of an organization in easy-to-understand terms. Failure to have a shared code of conduct can produce disastrous results in any organization. Over the past few decades, I have witnessed the sad decline in the effectiveness of public schools in the United States. This is seen not only in achievement test scores, but more so in a lack of order among the student population. Some fascinating research shows that in the early 1960s, one of the biggest problems in schools was students chewing gum in class. In recent years, the most significant problems are with students committing aggravated assault and using illegal drugs. While there may be some external factors that have contributed to this degeneration, I am convinced that one of the greatest mistakes ever made by school systems was the removal of the Ten Commandments and other religious references from display and discussion in the classrooms. My position is not based on any fundamental religious ideologies, but rather on my study of the concept of shared core values and operating principles. Here is how I view this.

For many years, every child was exposed in school to the Judeo-Christian concepts of the Ten Commandments and the Golden Rule—"Do unto others as you would have them do unto you." Also, they learned that they would experience significant consequences—positive or negative—for how well they followed the rules established by the school and other parts of society. They learned that if they violated school policy, they could be expelled. Following school, if they violated civil laws, they could be incarcerated. They also learned that if they proved themselves to be diligent students and concerned citizens in school, they stood a great chance of obtaining a good job after graduation, thereby having the means to generate personal wealth and security for their families.

Finally, one of the most life-changing concepts that students embraced was that all people were accountable ultimately for all of their actions to God, a power higher than themselves. Translated, this meant that little Johnny or Mary could anticipate that their deeds, good or bad, would generate a consequence in this life and in the life to come.

Exposure to these concepts created a set of shared behavioral expectations, beliefs, values, and a code of conduct adhered to by a majority of Americans for generations. At the micro level, this code of conduct provided a foundation for student diligence, a basic standard for conduct and morality in schools, respect for authority, and an accepted system of reward and punishment. At the macro level, these shared beliefs and core values were built upon by parents and local churches and synagogues that helped the entire American society galvanize into a powerful force with shared foundational values.

However, during the 1960s, individuals and groups began a concerted effort to remove all religion from the public school system. Unfortunately—or fortunately, depending on your position—these people were successful not only at "protecting" students from undue religious pressure, but also at removing most references to God, the Bible, and the Ten Commandments from school facilities.

During this same time period, school prayer was banned, which left little doubt in the minds of students that God and a code of absolute rights and wrongs were out and that a new code of conduct was in. This new code was an unwritten one based on the belief that each man, woman, boy, and girl was capable of developing his or her own standard of conduct.

In recent years, I have observed an effort to return some of the earlier foundations to our schools, but it is certainly a case of too little, too late for the countless thousands of people who survived their school years, and thus brought the creed of relativism into our workplaces. Thankfully, these people respond very favorably to company-sponsored initiatives to establish codes of shared values and principles. After all, they lived without them for years and witnessed the sad results for themselves.

I have learned that it is wise for an organization to expand its core values into operating principles to avoid misunderstandings and misinterpretation of the words themselves. For instance, in my own organization, the core value of honesty becomes a viable operating principle when our associates tell clients the truth about problems in their organizations instead of lying to perhaps gain a lucrative contract. The core value of caring becomes an operating principle as we show respect and concern for each person with whom we work, regardless of his or her position. This simple procedure of expanding our values into a set of positive behaviors has, in effect, created our company's culture, resulting in a good reputation with customers and others in our community. Written operating principles are designed to take ambiguity out of the core values. For example, people who work in our corporate offices understand that the core value of respect for others applies to our support staff as well as people outside our organization. This means that secretaries deserve to be included in decisions that directly affect their jobs, are spoken to politely, and are never subjected to sexual harassment.

Leaders should never assume that others automatically understand their standards or operating principles. It is wise to clarify these issues and present them in writing to customers, employees, and anyone else affected by them. With the operating principles in place, leaders avoid the danger of having an overzealous follower, like the one described at the beginning of this chapter, commit illegal or unethical acts to achieve the mission.

No organization has ever suffered from operating principles that were too clear, but many have died from lack of clarity.

Operating principles explain how to demonstrate the core values. They are the organization's character in action. These principles describe the way in which the core values are to be manifested on a daily basis. For example: *We will treat each employee with equal levels of respect. We will come to meetings on time. We will not interrupt each other during meetings. We will work to resolve conflicts cooperatively.* These principles should contain a balance of *we will* and *we will not* statements. While they may seem restrictive at first, they are exactly the opposite. Too often, organizations suffer from partial paralysis due to unclear operating principles. Without clear operating principles, meetings disintegrate into endurance sessions or grudge matches. Each member of the organization develops his own set of operating principles. Controlled chaos reigns. No organization has ever suffered from operating principles that were too clear, but many have died from lack of clarity.

Once clarified, operating principles become a powerful tool with which to build a productive organizational culture. One of my favorite manufacturing clients in West Virginia created the following set of core values and operating principles that are widely supported by employees. Their approach was to write statements that were somewhat broad and then to clarify them through extensive discussions with their employees. Here is their list:

We believe that every employee should:

1. *Conduct themselves in a positive manner.*
3. *Foster cooperation rather than confrontation.*
4. *Communicate in a positive and helpful manner—avoid propagating rumors and other forms of negative communication.*
5. *Promote doing the right thing instead of focusing on one's need to be right.*
6. *Recognize and appreciate others.*

The people who created this list are some of the strongest and most independent people I have ever met. They are also some of the most insightful. Both management and union employees recognized that clear core values and operating principles were a way to focus their energies on satisfying their customers rather than fighting against each other. In recent years, the value of their company has skyrocketed. I am not surprised. Core values attract and retain great leaders, faithful followers, and committed customers alike.

QUESTIONS AND REFLECTIONS

Business • Government • Ministry • Family • Personal

1. Do you know the core values of your organization? How are they used to guide the organization?

2. By which core values do you personally live?

3. Does your organization have clear operating principles for each part of its operation?

4. Are these principles followed and adhered to by all members of the organization?

5. How would increased focus on core values and operating principles benefit your organization? How would it benefit you personally?

CHAPTER 9

CASE STUDIES

DOW CORNING CORPORATION

From day one, the Dow Corning manufacturing plant in Elizabethtown, Kentucky, was plagued with problems. This unionized manufacturing site employed 260 people. The only thing worse than its productivity was the condition of its labor-management relationships. In the first few years of operation, the union went on strike twice, which cost the company nearly three million dollars. Obviously, something needed to change. But, what?

In early 1986, a group was formed to address the problem. This included Ralph Reed, the plant manager; Burnett Kelly, a corporate officer; Tony Singer, the plant human relations director; Dick Hazleton, the director of manufacturing and engineering, plus local union leaders. Together, they developed a masterful approach to change that transformed the Elizabethtown operation into a high-quality workplace. The process for change developed in Elizabethtown became a model for success at other Dow Corning plants and many other organizations throughout North America.

As part of the plan, my company was asked to help design a quality improvement and cultural change process at that location. This was no small task—considering that productivity, quality, and profitability were at an all-time low, and conflicts between labor and management were at an all-time high. My initial assessments showed that the plant was losing popularity with customers and corporate officers alike. If something did not change with its relationships and bottom-line performance, the entire operation was in very real danger of being shut down.

The leaders of the Elizabethtown operation began the change process by doing something that few of their predecessors had tried. They began to talk *with* their union counterparts and other employees instead of just talking at them. Each morning, top managers would walk through the plant, greet their coworkers, and ask them how they felt about their jobs, the company, and even the type of leadership they were receiving. Reed and Singer were determined to learn about the hopes and fears of other employees. At first, people were hesitant to speak freely about their concerns; they even avoided the "bosses." However, after several weeks went by, workers began to look forward to talking with their leaders. Once it became clear that these men genuinely cared about the organization and the people who worked there, employees began to respond with improved work performance. Why were these leaders successful? They discovered the power of becoming personally involved with their followers. They found areas of common interest and built upon them. They began to unleash the power of agreement. It never fails!

Through increased communication, the staff and employees at the Elizabethtown plant discovered that they had much more in common than in conflict. The primary concern they shared was the real possibility of the loss of their jobs if plant performance did not dramatically improve. The many years of low productivity and high levels of labor-management conflict had nearly convinced the corporate executives at Dow Corning to invest their resources in other locations. This gave managers and union employees a common enemy to rally against: unemployment! It also gave them a common goal: to improve their organization for the benefit of everyone who worked there.

However, even with the common challenge, it was obvious that members of the group would have a hard time forming a team. On the surface, the differences appeared too great. Many of the managers were highly educated urbanites sent from the corporate headquarters in Michigan to supervise the local workers. Most of the workers had been born and raised in the surrounding hills of Kentucky. A lot of employees had high school diplomas, but few had gone to college. There were other differences. Managers wore white shirts and dark ties. Workers wore blue uniforms. Managers spoke with northern accents, while many workers spoke with southern accents. Over the years, leaders and followers had gathered into two distinct cliques and tended to stay within them.

At times, the differences between the groups seemed insurmountable. But we continued to follow our plan for development and hoped for the best. We knew that communication was crucial to the success of the plan, so we took every opportunity to communicate the vision, mission, and desired values to everyone who worked at the plant. The leaders continually talked about what type of culture they wanted to see there and how everyone would benefit from the change.

While much of this information was transmitted during informal communication with employees, the plant leaders also formally declared their commitment to improve the operation. In response to the challenges before them, they developed a comprehensive mission statement that encompassed their six most foundational business components, their operating philosophy and principles, and their total commitment to teamwork.

The Dow Corning leaders took the time necessary to ensure that their statement was written in a way that made it easy for all employees to understand, retain, and apply it to their daily jobs. They called the following their mission statement, but it is actually much more than that. It includes *what* they wanted to achieve, *how* they wanted to achieve it, and *which* business issues were most critical. *Elizabethtown Mission Statement: [to] demonstrate continuous improvement in team excellence as a high-quality, low-cost supplier who satisfies our customers' needs in a safe, productive, and waste-free manner.*

For months, company leaders would recite this statement to employees every chance that they had. Soon, employees were able to remember these primary business concerns, which became known as the Key Six. They were safety, quality, cost, productivity, supply [to customers], and reduction of waste. Next, each employee was able to use these six concerns to analyze and solve complex problems that previously would have halted production. They soon were able to make management-level decisions by focusing on what was truly important to the plant's success—the Key Six.

Within six months, it was obvious that employees understood the mission and had embraced the vision of a unified workplace. However, embracing a concept of unity and putting it into practice are two different things. So, the next part of our plan was to build productive relationships among the 260 managers and employees. Remember that these were the same people whose work performances had contributed to the organization's bottom-line problems and whose attitudes had fostered the complete lack of respect between labor and management.

A three-way informal partnership between management, local union leaders, and Molitor International was formed to create training programs for all employees. Topics included leadership, teamwork, communication, and team problem solving.

In an initial effort to build productive relationships, we designed a team-building workshop that I would facilitate for management and their union counterparts. At the opening of our first session, I silently questioned the wisdom of such a gathering. The managers all sat on one side of the training room while the union leaders sat on the other. There was no eye contact. There were no smiles. It looked grim, but at that point there was no turning back.

In our first exercise, I asked participants to locate a person in the room about whom they knew very little. The assignment was to interview that person using some *nonwork related* questions that I provided. The participants immediately responded to my instructions with disbelief. They looked shocked to think that they were being asked to cross the invisible barrier that ran down the center of the room and actually engage in positive dialogue with someone from the "other side." It was amusing to watch grown men try to cope with the uncomfortable situation. Each person tried in vain to disappear from sight. Some shuffled their feet, some cleaned nonexistent spots on their glasses, others suddenly developed an intense interest in the notebooks before them and buried their faces in its pages. I felt as though I was the chaperon at a junior high school dance watching as the boys and girls breathlessly waited for someone to ask for the first dance.

Finally, one brave soul rose from his seat and called a cool invitation to a former adversary across the room. Mercifully, the invitation was accepted; together, they walked from the room to a quiet place in the hallway.

The ice was broken! Slowly, other managers and union leaders began to form pairs and ask each other the simple series of questions. They spoke about issues of importance to their lives outside of the plant. After a brief period of guarded conversation, they began to share more openly about families, hobbies, personal goals, and the high points of their lives. I watched in grateful amazement as men pulled family photographs from their wallets and showed them to their new friends.

Although I had given instructions for the interviewing assignment to be completed in thirty minutes, they did not seem to care about the time limit. Once they started, these people did not want to stop talking with each other! When I finally brought the entire group back together, I was amazed at the transformation that had taken place. They were smiling, joking, and were much more at peace than when the workshop began. Many of them actually sat with the person whom they had interviewed, which destroyed the invisible barrier in the room. When they had reassembled, I asked them to identify common interests they had discovered during the interviews. What followed was an absolute clinic on how to build a team.

A 40 percent reduction in final rejects sent their quality ratings skyrocketing.

Union leaders and managers alike divulged issues that gave true meaning to their lives. They talked about their spouses and children, their faith in God, love of their country, and the desire for financial security. They shared their goals of a productive retirement and peace of mind. Many excitedly spoke about how they enjoyed fishing, hunting, golf, and other forms of recreation. By the end of the exercise, these fine people discovered the truth that had been hidden from them for so long: They had a great deal in common, and by agreeing to work together they could achieve both their personal and corporate goals.

This one simple exercise opened a new era for their organization. As management and union employees grew closer to one another, they implemented other innovative ideas to help the plant become a model for the rest of the corporation. During the next few years, we actually trained each employee at the plant in a full range of interpersonal skills, including leadership, teamwork, communications, listening, trust building, and problem solving. These new skills laid a foundation for open dialogue and positive relationships to develop among workers at every level. As trust developed, so did more open lines of communication. More open communication resulted in better problem identification, analysis, and resolution. This, in turn, resulted in improved work performance and a much more positive work environment.

THE RESULTS

As the months passed, the hard work began to produce some dramatic results. I had the pleasure of consulting with the Elizabethtown operation for over seven years. During this time, their plant operated for more than three million person-hours without a lost-time injury. They delivered products to customers on or before the delivery date more than 96 percent of the time. The operation's fixed costs were reduced by over 7 percent. The rate of productivity rose by more than 6 percent. Manufacturing process waste was reduced by more than 25 percent. A 40 percent reduction in final rejects sent their quality ratings skyrocketing. As a wonderful by-product of this success, the vast majority of employees and managers actually enjoyed coming to work. They were proud to be part of something so positive!

This case study should motivate every champion of change. It is important to remember that the Elizabethtown plant did not import a handpicked group of homogenous superstars to turn the operation around. Instead, they produced these dramatic results with the same group of employees and managers who worked there during their worst years. This proves beyond a shadow of a doubt that in the proper environment, managers and employees can change, grow, and prosper.

COVENANT HEALTH-CARE SYSTEM

My analysis of Covenant Hospital's effectiveness began at 3:00 A.M. on March 17, 1997, in a very unexpected way. I received a phone call that my seventy-five-year-old father had suffered a life threatening heart attack and was being rushed to the hospital. As if in a dream, I sleepily dressed and drove the forty miles to meet other tearful family members assembled in the hospital's waiting room.

In the weeks that followed, I learned much about the importance of health-care professionals and the profound impact they have on our lives. What I did not know at the time was that my company would be hired by Covenant to assist them in developing their new corporate culture. What began as a tragedy ultimately became one of the most exciting health-care projects that we have ever undertaken.

At the time of my father's heart attack, the name of the hospital was Saint Luke's Health Care Association. A new entity, Covenant Hospital, was about to be created from the merger between Saint Luke's and Saginaw General Hospital. Each had an impressive history of providing quality care to its customers for over one hundred years. They officially merged on July 1, 1998, to form one of the largest health-care organizations in Michigan. Combined, they employ four thousand people in a wide variety of positions. Because I had spent many years living in Saginaw, I knew that these hospitals were great providers of quality care. All four of my children were born in Saginaw General Hospital's birthing center, and other family members had minor surgeries at both hospitals. However, I had never seen their talents put to the ultimate test until the day of my father's heart attack.

Initial tests showed several life-threatening blockages in the main arteries of his heart. The situation called for quadruple bypass surgery. After the lengthy operation was performed, my father was taken to a recovery room. We breathed a collective sigh of relief as a smiling hospital chaplain entered the waiting room and informed us of Dad's progress. As the chaplain departed, we released our pent-up fears with smiles and tears. It was such a relief to think that everything would be fine. What we did not know was that the ordeal was far from over.

Approximately twenty minutes later, the chaplain reappeared at the waiting-room door. This time, his face was ashen, and he explained in hushed tones that something was terribly wrong. My father had been rushed back into surgery. There, the surgeon had to reopen his chest cavity to stop some internal bleeding and to address some new complications. The hospital staff prepared us for the worst. My mother, other family members, and I prayerfully waited as tense minutes turned into exhausting hours. Finally, at 8:30 P.M., the surgeon was once again finished, and they moved my father into another recovery area adjacent to the operating room. I later learned that this fine surgeon had canceled two nonemergency surgeries scheduled for that day in order to stay with my father during this critical time.

What followed the second surgery was one of the most stressful times that the Molitor family has ever endured. Dad's life hung on the edge of eternity for days. He was placed on extensive life support systems, as he was unable to breathe for himself. Nurses in the cardiac care intensive care unit (CCICU) who watched over him twenty-four hours a day seemed like angels dressed in blue scrub uniforms. Although my father was unconscious, they encouraged us to visit him. During these brief visits, the nurses were both kind and competent. Their confident actions and gentle words brought comfort to my grieving mother, who practically lived at the hospital for the next twenty-one days.

Following the surgery, I discovered that the hospital's excellence extended well beyond just the operating and recovery rooms. For example, at one point in the ordeal, we had been awake for nearly twenty-four hours and could barely keep our eyes opened. Concerned staff members offered to let my mother and other family members rest in some unoccupied hospital beds rather than spend the entire night in the lobby waiting area. Their offers of clean towels and extra blankets proved to me one thing: These people truly cared!

The following weeks brought me into contact with hospital administrators, doctors, nurses, cafeteria staff, and volunteers. With very few exceptions, these people showed tremendous competence and sincere concern. Quality care and top-notch customer service clearly were part of their culture. I am thrilled to report that twenty-one days after his heart attack, my father was able to return home with a new appreciation for health-care professionals and life itself.

During one of my visits to the hospital, I arranged to meet with the chief executive officer, Spencer Maidlow, and the chief operating officer, Bill Heath, to see how they had achieved such a fine operation (sorry, no pun intended). I also wanted to thank them personally for doing such a fine job caring for my father. As we spoke, I was not surprised to learn that their success had been no accident; it was the result of careful planning and hard work. Also, I learned that the only thing constant about the health-care business is constant change! During a subsequent meeting, I was invited to assist Covenant with their merger plans by creating and implementing a long-term developmental process.

Once the project was underway, my primary contact at Covenant was their director of organizational effectiveness, Bill Parsons. Bill shared with me that the organizational development history of each hospital was similar, even though each hospital had used different methods. I learned that Saint Luke's had been involved in training and development during the previous six years. Saginaw General Hospital also had undertaken numerous change initiatives over the years to optimize their performance. This background information was extremely helpful to know as we designed the plan to unify their four thousand employees. I was amazed at the amount of work that people at Covenant had to do to make the merger a success. Although their cultures were similar, some major problems needed to be addressed. These employees, who had been competitors for many years, were now expected to work together. Also, because each hospital had been essentially a full-service provider, there were duplicate departments, units, and staff positions. Somehow, each of these issues had to be addressed in a manner consistent with Covenant's new vision and values. I was pleased to discover that the leadership at Covenant had done an excellent job of putting their vision, mission, and statement of values in writing and used this information to guide decisions about the merger. The following are Covenant Hospital's actual statements of vision, mission, and values.

OUR VISION STATEMENT

A promise of caring—A commitment to service

OUR MISSION STATEMENT

We bring together the people, the caring cultures, and the values of our founding hospitals into a renewed commitment to building an accessible, comprehensive health-care network serving Michigan. In fulfilling this commitment, we are guided by the following principles:

> WE commit to providing exceptional care through competence, compassion, and spiritual and ethical values.
>
> WE maintain financial strength while encouraging risk taking and exploration: Creating solutions to anticipate and meet the changing needs of our environment.

WE believe alignment and integration of our corporate entities, teams, physician, and providers of care are required for the success of our network.

WE support an empowered and accountable workforce that embraces change in the pursuit of excellence.

WE reach out to the communities we serve through the development of health-care enterprises, wellness programs, and the provision of care to our communities.

WE support research, education, and technology, and have an evolving role in helping our communities to improve their health.

WE value a workforce that is diverse and representative of the communities we serve, and we strive to understand and appreciate our diversity.

OUR VALUES STATEMENT—WE CARE

Working together—We understand that teamwork is the foundation to our success. We diligently work together as a team while balancing work and home life.

Excellence—We strive through empowerment to do and be the very best in all of our endeavors.

Customer service—We recognize that our very existence is to serve. We commit to an unsurpassed level of service to all our customers.

Accountability—We are responsible to our communities, our organization, and to each other.

Respect—We display a high regard for the personal dignity, diversity, and the uniqueness of those served and those serving. We treat all others as we want to be treated.

Enthusiasm—We project a spirit and attitude that is positive and optimistic. We seek to find good in all people and all situations.

The next step in the developmental process was to communicate both cultural and directional information to all employees. This was accomplished during a series of cultural awareness sessions. During these sessions, employees were treated to presentations, videotapes, and printed materials that addressed past accomplishments of the two separate hospitals. Also, employees were told how Covenant's leaders viewed the future for the new unified organization. One of the most powerful parts of the sessions dealt with behavioral expectations for leaders and followers alike. This list of attitudes and actions left little doubt that Covenant wanted to create a team atmosphere in which trust and mutual respect were more than just words on paper. Most employees left the sessions with a mixture of optimism and anxiety. This was to be expected because in the merger, many of their responsibilities, working conditions, compensation, and reporting relationships would be changing within the next few months. Also, these were mature individuals who realized that merging two existing organizations into a new megahospital was easier said than done.

Following the sessions, we needed to create a customized, long-term plan for education and training. This was done to ensure that the values and expectations presented at the cultural awareness sessions would become reality in the daily work lives of employees. The logistics of involving so many people in the different components of training complicated the task. Soon, however, Bill Parsons and I had designed the training plan and had begun to implement it systematically. The plan essentially follows the chapters of this book, so I won't rewrite it here.

Our plan for Covenant included training in the topics of leadership, teamwork, communication, listening, managing change through proper employee involvement, plus many others. Also, my associates and I provided the executive management team with personalized leadership coaching to assist them with their many challenges. As with all organizational change efforts, we observed that some leaders and employees made swift adjustments to the new work environment, while others needed more time. We were undaunted by this fact because of our firm conviction that any organization can deal successfully with drastic change as long as its leaders are willing to establish and follow a long-term plan.

THE RESULTS OF THE MERGER

As of this writing, Covenant is in the early stages of adjusting to all of the changes, so it is too early for many specific assessments. However, I am pleased to report that Covenant's patients and their families are still enjoying the excellent customer service that each hospital had provided earlier. This is much more than just my opinion. Covenant regularly participates in a nationally recognized customer satisfaction survey that measures their performance against other hospitals throughout the United States. In recent months, they have scored in the top 20 percent overall, and their nursing component is consistently in the top 10 percent of hospitals involved in the survey.

Also, the merger has produced some innovative methods to improve both performance effectiveness and customer satisfaction. For example, Covenant preregisters patients to facilitate a streamlined patient intake process and to eliminate a long waiting period for customers. Each employee wears a nametag with his or her picture on it for easy identification by patients. The hospital accepted a suggestion to install individual phones and televisions in patient rooms to give people a greater sense of independence and personal control during their stays. The list of innovations that Covenant employees have developed is impressive and seemingly unending. This is truly an organization that, as a result of the merger, is capitalizing on the power found in agreement.

SOME FINAL THOUGHTS ON THE CASE STUDIES

I selected these two case studies to show that widely diverse organizations can reach their peak performances if they follow the proper procedures. In both cases, the organization's leaders were men and women of vision who were committed to change. They clearly identified their organization's purpose and direction, then established core values and clear expectations of behavior for everyone. Finally, they designed a plan for educating and training that involved people throughout their entire operation. Leadership was willing to invest financially in the development of the critical skills necessary for employees to serve customers and manage change in the future. They planned their work. They worked their plan. Their plan worked. So can yours.

What about the future of these companies . . . or any other that has moved forward with a developmental process? Will organizations like the Dow Corning Elizabethtown manufacturing plant and Covenant Health-care System always enjoy this kind of success? My answer to this question is yes, but it comes with one condition: If the organization remains committed to excellence and its people continue to follow the pattern that brought them to this level, they will continue to succeed.

So can you.

QUESTIONS AND REFLECTIONS

Business • Government • Ministry • Family • Personal

1. How has your organization changed over the past five years?

2. What areas of your organization are more effective now than in the past?

3. What areas of your organization are less effective now than in the past?

4. What caused the change?

CHAPTER 10

YOU *CAN* GET THERE FROM HERE

From the time I was a boy, I have enjoyed hunting and fishing in Michigan. Whenever I travel into new territory, I always carry a complete survival kit that includes a compass. Despite these precautions, I have wandered for hours on occasion before I finally returned to camp. In those times of being directionally impaired—OK, I admit that I was lost—I realized that I needed to know more than just where I wanted to go. That was the easy part. Obviously, I wanted to go back to camp. However, the more difficult part of the equation was that I also needed to know *where I was starting from*.

This same problem faces today's organizational leaders who have little difficulty determining that they want to achieve excellence as providers of products or services. However, like people lost in the woods, these same organizations often embark on journeys to improve quality, productivity, customer relations, or teamwork without knowing their starting points.

I am amazed at the number of companies willing to spend huge amounts of time and money on programs that they don't

THE MOLITOR DEVELOPMENTAL PROCESS

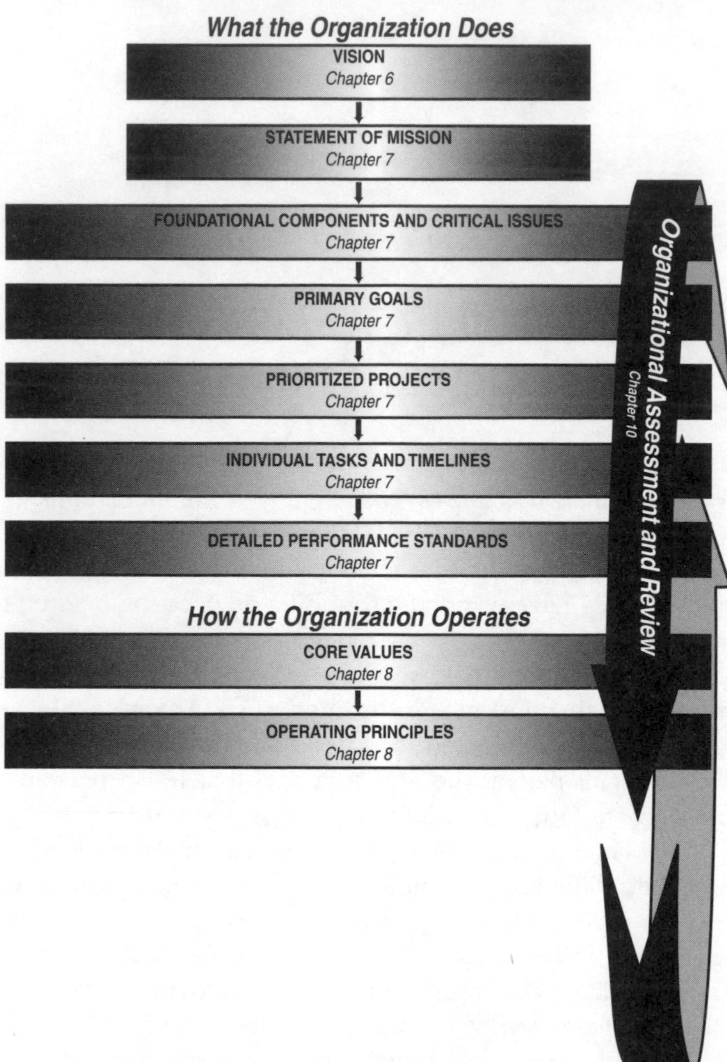

need, and yet they are unwilling to invest relatively small sums on an organizational assessment to determine what they do need.

The following scenario from a newspaper column I wrote a few years ago will illustrate my point. This conversation took place between two cross-country runners.

> HARRY: Hey Rick, this is the third time we've passed this same tree. I think we are lost!
>
> RICK: Are you kidding? We're making great progress. Look at the sweat we've worked up! Besides, I saw another runner heading in that direction, so the finish line is probably just over that hill. Let's go!
>
> HARRY: Wait a minute. Shouldn't we figure out where we are now, before we just take off running?
>
> RICK: No way! We can't afford to waste time on that. The competition is probably ahead of us now. Besides, who cares where we are now? Just run faster and we'll get there!

These runners are similar to many people who want to make positive changes but are unsure of how to do it. Hard work and sweat are not necessarily indications of progress. Millions of dollars and thousands of hours are wasted each year as leaders of organizations race for a prize called *excellence* without ever reaching the finish line. Why? They have never done a complete assessment of all the different aspects of their companies. In effect, they do not know where they are now. This is especially true in the area of human relations. There is a tremendous need to determine strengths and weaknesses in this crucial area *before* making a change in organizational structure, personnel, or trying to improve performance with a new program of any sort.

The concept of assessment and evaluation is certainly not foreign to most organizations. It is common for leaders to evaluate parts of their organizations on an annual basis. Accounting audits, physical inventory, and marketing plans are some of the most common components routinely evaluated for their effectiveness. If it makes good sense to evaluate these individual parts of the organization, then it also makes sense for leaders to assess the condition of employee morale and the quality of interpersonal relationships throughout the organization. These areas are often neglected, with serious consequences to both the organization's culture and bottom-line performance.

We must remember that every change in an organization impacts its people, and its people impact every change. They either will promote or resist change depending on their level of commitment to the process. And their commitment to the process is largely determined by their relationships with others in their organization, especially their leaders.

We must remember that every change in an organization impacts its people, and its people impact every change.

I recall some studies done on organizations targeted by union organizers. The number-one issue that determined whether employees voted for or against joining the union was their relationships with their first-line supervisors. Isn't that amazing? It was not wages or working conditions, but the employee's personal relationship with supervision.

The underlying issues here are found in each person's inherent need to feel secure, respected, and valued by others. Supervisors and managers who fail to lead others with kindness, civility, and professionalism often find their employees looking to other institutions, such as unions, to satisfy these basic needs. Too many managers and business owners know intimate details about their company's inventory levels, current returns on investment, and complex production schedules, yet they are oblivious to the condition of human relations within their organizations.

THE ORGANIZATIONAL ASSESSMENT

Leaders who are serious about change must determine the condition of relationships in their company *before* they begin any significant initiative. The power of agreement is released in two ways: first, by discovering areas where two or more people can agree and building upon those issues, and, second, by discovering issues where two or more people disagree and then resolving the disagreements. An organizational assessment can be used to discover both of these areas.

An assessment may be done in many ways, with each having its own pluses and minuses. It must be remembered that an assessor's primary mission is to obtain perceptions of strengths and weaknesses from people at all levels of an organization and then accurately report findings to that organization's leaders. Assessment may be informal, using an organization's internal personnel and resources, or may be completed by outside experts using a very systematic process. Also, an organization may choose to interview a small sampling of its employees or may include all personnel in the process. Informal surveys completed in-house have the benefit of being completed rapidly and generally at a lower cost than one using external resources.

However, the drawback with this approach is twofold. First, the in-house personnel may not have sufficient credibility with employees to succeed, and workers may not trust the interviewer to remain impartial when the organization is criticized. The second potential problem concerns interviewers who are not properly trained; they may miss critical cues from people questioned. I have learned that what employees are *not* willing to discuss is just as important as what they are willing to discuss during an assessment interview. Therefore, it makes me very nervous to have a novice attempt to assess an organization's human relations climate.

The assessment process is more difficult than it may appear. A human relations assessment is much more complex than other standard inventory procedures in the corporate world. The assessor is doing much more than just counting cans on a shelf. Indeed, he or she is probing the uncharted depths of human thoughts and emotions. Therefore, if an organization has the ability to invest the time and financial resources, it is always best to have an impartial professional perform the assessment.

There are some exceptions to this. For example, in relatively small, cohesive groups such as a family, one of the leaders—in this case, a parent—may simply call a meeting to discuss each member's perception of the state of the family. Small, closely held businesses also may be assessed in this manner. However, where there is existing strife, mistrust, or unresolved conflict in families, businesses, local churches, or other organizations, it is better to have someone from the outside assist with gathering the information. In large organizations, such as business, industry, or government, this informal approach would never work. To be effective in this environment, the assessors not only must be credible, competent, and unbiased, but they also must be *perceived* to have these qualities by the people to be interviewed.

Through the years, my associates and I have interviewed thousands of people using a systematic approach that gathers information from nearly 100 percent of an organization's employees. Our approach is time consuming and tedious, but it is the most effective way to obtain a complete picture of what is happening inside an organization. It's like a doctor who is attempting to diagnose a patient with internal problems. If the doctor is wise, he will not be satisfied to look only at the outside of a patient and then recommend treatment. Instead, he will send the patient for X rays and other advanced methods of determining what is actually happening inside the body. A proper diagnosis usually results in a healthy patient; conversely, a surface diagnosis may cause the patient to suffer, or even die. So it is with the assessment of an organization. You must look below the surface, into the depths of the organization, to understand truly what is causing its successes and failures. I am convinced that this type of "X-ray" assessment can occur only when face-to-face interviews are conducted with the vast majority of employees at all levels. I strongly oppose computerized surveys that attempt to gather input from a "representative" sample of people. With all due respect to the world's statisticians, this is a very dangerous method of determining what employees are thinking. People differ from department to department and from one work shift to another.

It is much like the story of the blind men who attempted to describe an elephant by touching it in different spots. One man touched the elephant's side and described it as a wall. Another touched its trunk and described it as a snake. Still another man touched the elephant's leg and described it as a tree. Each was firmly convinced that he had a complete understanding about elephants. What these men really needed was someone to help them combine all of their perceptions. This would provide them with a full picture of what an elephant really looks like.

Countless times, modern-day blind men in the corporate world have reenacted this story. These people honestly believe that they have grasped the cause of their organization's problems when, in fact, they see only a small part of it. One man brings a defective part into a manufacturing meeting and declares that quality is the problem. Another brings in a report about a customer complaint and is certain that customer service is the place to invest the company's resources. Still another overhears two employees arguing in the hallway and states emphatically that their problem is a lack of teamwork. The impact of these different perceptions can be profound. Why? Because the way you define a problem will dictate how you solve it. This organization may invest hundreds of thousands of dollars in product quality, customer service, or a team-building program without ever confirming that the approach will solve the problems. If the organization has limited resources to invest into any of these efforts, then the program that has the backing of the highest-ranking manager or the most convincing orator will end up with the funds. A careful assessment will help avoid the blind-man syndrome and reveal the entire picture.

HOW IT IS DONE

After a lot of trial and error, my staff and I have found an effective method of collecting assessment data. We coordinate our assessment work with one person inside each organization, someone with access and sufficient authority to create a master schedule for the employee interviews. Creating this schedule is a significant undertaking, especially in larger organizations, but with proper planning it can be achieved with a minimum of disruption for the company. It is best to schedule the interviews from sixty to ninety minutes in length. Also, we begin at the foundational level of the organization and work toward upper levels of management. Generally, in small groups of five to seven people, we interview nonsupervisory employees from the same work area. This saves time and money for the organization. Also, we have learned that this level of employees has similar perceptions of the organization's strengths and weaknesses.

When we reach the first level of supervision, we begin to conduct individual interviews, and we will continue in this mode until we complete our final interview with the organization's highest official. Using this method, we accomplish two powerful things: First, we have a complete understanding of the human relations issues that face the organization. In a relatively short period of time, we have become experts in that company's past and present, which puts us in a unique position to help design its future. Also, since my staff conducts the interviews with virtually the entire workforce, we already have begun to develop a relationship with them. This relationship, and the trust that it fosters, helps these employees to be open and relaxed when they attend our training classes, which often follow an assessment.

THE HIDDEN BENEFITS OF AN ASSESSMENT

There is more to a properly done assessment than just gathering data about an organization. I have found that assessments not only uncover the real strengths and weaknesses of an organization, but also unify and prepare people for change. I believe that at least 50 percent of the value gained from an assessment comes from the fact that each person involved develops ownership in the change process. They know that their input will be used to help move the organization in a new direction, and they want to help shape their own futures.

It is important to remember two things about assessments: First, we feel ownership for things that we help build. Second, we take care of what we own. Therefore, meaningful involvement in an assessment increases people's sense of ownership in the organizational change process. For this reason, it is wise to involve as many people as possible during an assessment. As a result, they will own it and care for it for the duration of the change process.

ASSESSMENT TOPICS

The following is a list of topics that we normally use to assess a wide variety of clients in business, government, health-care, and religious organizations. These are some of the most universal causes for relationship breakdown and low organizational effectiveness.

Mission, Foundational Components, and Critical Issues

What is the mission of the organization? Why does it exist? What are the foundational components and critical issues to be addressed in order to achieve the mission?

These are the foundational questions of any assessment. If leaders and followers fail to agree on the purpose and direction of their organization, they can never succeed.

Core Values and Operating Principles

What are the core values of the organization? What does this organization stand for? Do you consistently adhere to the core values?

It is crucial to determine if the core values are universally understood and accepted—also, if followers are able to align their performances with the operating principles and the foundational core values?

Trust and Openness

What is the current level of trust and openness in the organization? Is leadership credible? Has sufficient time been spent developing relationships that foster trust?

A lack of trust will slow the process of change to a crawl. A lack of openness will cause decisions to be made without sufficient facts or support from some members of the organization.

Leader Effectiveness

How productive is the organization? Is the mission being accomplished? Are followers motivated or demotivated by interaction with leaders? Do leaders have sufficient skills, knowledge, and motivation to productively inspire followers?

Organizational change begins with leadership. This is one of the most crucial areas to assess correctly.

FOLLOWER EFFECTIVENESS

How well do followers interact with leaders? Do they resist change? Are they prepared technically and interpersonally to be productive members of the organization? Do they demonstrate a strong commitment to the mission?

While leaders have the initial responsibility for change, followers must be prepared to work closely with leaders. Much of the teaching done on the topic of leadership is unbalanced and potentially damaging to long-term relationships between leaders and followers. It puts the entire burden for change on the shoulders of leaders and permits less-than-complete commitment from followers. There is a shared responsibility that must be understood by both leaders and followers to optimize the process of change.

COMMUNICATION AND LISTENING SKILLS

How effective is the communication process within the organization? When people speak, do they achieve complete understanding and build positive relationships? Is vital information lost during the communication process?

People tend to spend a great deal of time talking, but often fail to communicate effectively. Also, improved listening skills can be the catalyst for significant improvements in organizational effectiveness and personal relationships.

INFORMATION FLOW

Does the organization have methods and systems in place to keep people properly informed? Are leaders aware of their followers' concerns, problems, and suggestions? Are followers informed of critical issues, challenges, and successes that the organization has experienced?

An effective organizational assessment will determine whether vital information is flowing to the right people in a timely manner. It can pinpoint constrictions, gaps, and redundancies in the system.

INTERDEPENDENCE

Do people recognize that they need one another's contributions to achieve the mission? Do members of the organization know what function the other levels, areas, and individuals actually perform?

An organization is like a body, with each person serving as a different part. Often those who are "hands" fail to understand that they need the "feet" in the organization to succeed.

MORALE

What is the current level of morale in the company or group being assessed? Does it differ from area to area? Are leaders motivated, encouraged, energized, and committed to the mission? Is the morale of followers different than that of leaders? If so, why?

Morale is never a stand-alone issue in any organization. It increases or decreases because of people's reactions to changing conditions. The assessment uncovers the primary causes of the current levels of morale.

POSITIVE REINFORCEMENT

How do people know when they have performed well? Is acceptable and ideal performance recognized? In what ways is it recognized? Is there a formal or informal method of rewarding people? If so, is it consistent?

Often, we fail to acknowledge good performance in those around us. This lack of encouragement eventually creates a "What's the use?" mentality in even the best performers.

CORRECTIVE FEEDBACK

How does someone know when he has performed poorly? Is unacceptable performance recognized and corrected? Is assistance given when someone cannot perform up to the stated standards? Is discipline administered fairly and equally?

Addressing poor performance is one of the most uncomfortable, and yet vital, aspects of organizational development. During the assessment, corrective feedback methods are analyzed for both consistency and effectiveness.

PERFORMANCE ENHANCEMENT PROCESS

Is there a formal system in place to develop the skills of personnel in the organization? How is it administered? Are training, coaching, and counseling available to those who want or need it?

Often, we try to develop filet mignon employees on a hamburger budget. Or we expect our managers' and employees' performances to improve automatically without a systematic development plan in place. Remember that poor performance is easy to achieve by doing nothing, but excellence must be planned.

APPROACH TO PROBLEM SOLVING

How are problems addressed? Do a few high-level people try to solve the majority of the problems and make most of the decisions for the organization? Is a systematic approach used to address problems? Have all members of the organization been trained in problem solving?

All organizations need to solve problems quickly and accurately. The assessment should give a complete overview of the organization's approach and effectiveness in this vital area.

A WORD OF CAUTION

An organizational assessment can be like cleaning out a teenager's closet—you never know what you will discover.

You may find some hidden treasures as well as things that are not very pleasant. Often, we find that our assessments identify certain managers or supervisors who are having a negative impact on their followers. It is very common for employees to mention managers who are harsh, negative, and/or autocratic. In these instances, it is vital to remember that an assessment is not intended as an individual performance review. Instead, it is designed to identify positive and negative trends within the organization.

I have had to remind some top managers of this fact after an assessment pinpointed a particular supervisor who was having a negative impact on the workforce. The reason for this restraint is simple. When an organization has poor managers or supervisors, there are only three possibilities for how they became such liabilities: The organization hired them that way, allowed them to get that way, or made them that way. There is no legitimate way that top management can avoid responsibility for the actions of mid-level managers and first-line supervisors. Often, managers who receive the worst evaluations during an assessment are those who were rewarded previously by top management for their harsh approach to employee relations. Now, these same managers are instructed to involve and empower their subordinates rather than intimidate them. Unfortunately, their past behaviors have created a negative reputation for them, and they must work very hard to overcome it.

The point here is simple. The supervisors and managers who helped build an organization using the negative tactics of the past deserve an opportunity to change. They are not to be discarded. They are not to be bypassed unless they refuse to change with the times. An assessment is an ideal opportunity to discover what needs to be done differently for the organization to become more competitive. Unless the assessment exposes some type of gross negligence or immoral or illegal activity on the part of a leader, then it is also an ideal opportunity to clear everyone's slate—forgive, forget, and move forward together.

YOU *CAN* GET THERE FROM HERE

Once the organizational assessment has been completed and analyzed, the time of aimless wandering is over. This information, when coupled with the vision, mission, and core values, provides direction for the journey to the camp called Excellence. To arrive there with a minimum of wasted time and backtracking, organizational leaders now must develop a comprehensive plan.

QUESTIONS AND REFLECTIONS

Business • Government • Ministry • Family • Personal

1. When was the last time your organization had a complete assessment of its strengths and weaknesses? What were the results?

2. Are leaders of your organization in touch with the concerns of followers? What is the impact of your answer?

3. What are some organizational blind spots that your leaders may have?

4. How are complaints, questions, and concerns handled within your organization?

5. What are your personal strengths and weaknesses? What are your possible blind spots?

CHAPTER 11

THE POWER OF A PLAN

"This is terrible!" moaned the myopic manager. "We can't let the employees hear these assessment results. There are too many problems! What will they think?"

This was one top manager's initial response to the results of his organization's assessment. Until then, the assessment process had gone according to plan. In our initial meetings, this manager said all of the right things about wanting to change the company's operation to achieve excellence. In a preassessment memo to all employees, he even urged them to be completely honest with their thoughts about the company. During interviews, employees seemed genuinely pleased to have an opportunity to identify the strengths and weaknesses of their organization. With very few exceptions, they were extremely honest and gave us their ideas in a very professional manner. My team and I finished our final interviews right on schedule and were satisfied that we now had the basis for some solid recommendations to the company.

THE MOLITOR DEVELOPMENTAL PROCESS

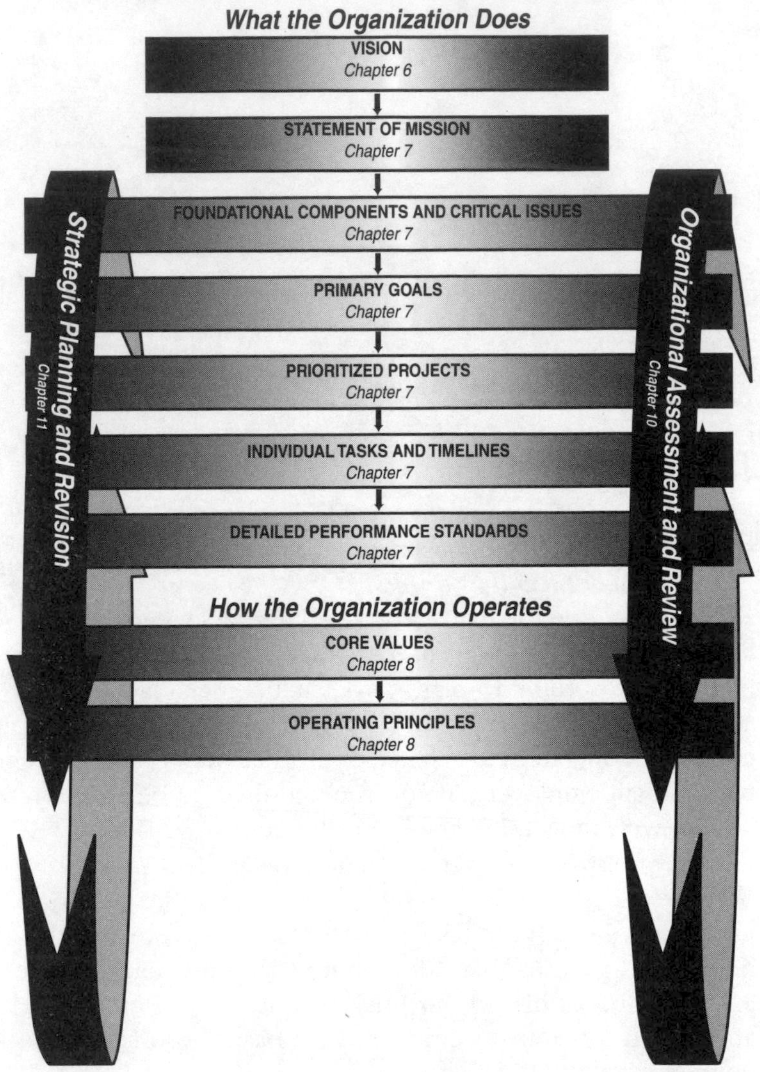

Following the interviews, we flew home and spent the next few days compiling the assessment data. Soon, our assessment report was completed and I returned to communicate my findings, first to the manager and his staff, then to the rest of the employees. The report was fairly typical of many of today's companies. It showed strengths as well as employee concerns about poor communication and autocratic management practices. I expected company management to receive the information with some minor regrets, but then move quickly on to plan for the future.

As I shared the assessment results with the top manager and his staff, I soon learned just how wrong my expectations really were. Even though the report mentioned nothing that could not be addressed, the top manager still seemed frantic. The fact that his employees viewed the organization as less than perfect sent him into an irrational panic. He was petrified at the thought of presenting the results to the three hundred employees who had assembled in the company's cramped meeting hall. I was just as petrified at the thought of not presenting the results to the employees, since I had promised during interviews that they would hear the same report as their managers. After the top manager's initial outburst, we all sat in painful silence. The stillness was broken when the top manager mumbled again: *"What will they think?"*

This happened more than a decade ago, but I still remember vividly the turmoil of the day. My response to his question was clear. After recovering from the shock of his reaction, I told him that the employees will probably think three things. First, they will think that we accurately recorded what they said during the interviews. Second, they will think that their leader actually cares enough to listen to them. And, third, they will think that their managers are going to solve the problems that the employees have known about all along.

I finally convinced him that his employees wouldn't be shocked, discouraged, or quit because of the company's problems—especially since they were the ones who identified them in the first place. We eventually made our way to the meeting hall, and I began to present the assessment results. I couldn't help but notice that the poor manager winced each time I read about a problem area. The reaction of the employees was quite the opposite. They neither winced nor gloated over their company's shortcomings. Instead, they sat quietly and occasionally nodded in agreement as the report was read.

At the conclusion of the session, one employee stood and addressed the red-faced manager, who braced himself, expecting the worst. His fears were unfounded. The employee simply thanked him for commissioning the assessment. He further explained that he and his coworkers were glad to know that management was finally going to address some of the long-term problems, and pledged his support of the effort. As other employees left the room, many of them came to the manager and echoed their coworker's comments. When the room was finally empty, the manger sat in silence for several minutes. On his face was the look of someone who had taken one too many rides on a roller coaster.

We eventually moved the planning process forward and provided some training for his employees, but this project never came close to reaching its potential. The reason was quite simple: This manager spent more time trying to justify the shortcomings of his organization than fixing them.

Fortunately, this manager's response to an assessment is not the norm. While it is very common for most top leaders to feel some disappointment when negative results are revealed, most want to move quickly into the next phase: addressing the problems. Over the years, I have witnessed a full range of reactions to assessment reports. Managers have expressed everything from tears when the report was bad to laughter when the report turned out better than they had been anticipated.

While reactions to an assessment report will vary, one thing is constant: the importance of knowing the truth about one's organization. Plans for success must be founded upon truth. They must not be founded upon rumors, assumptions, guesses, or even what proved to be true in someone else's company, church, or family. A properly performed assessment will reveal truth that, in turn, will provide the foundation for an organization's plan for change. Today, our supervisors and managers have significantly different roles than that of their predecessors. With all of the downsizing, combining of departments, increased government regulations, and community relations activities that have become part of a manager's ever-expanding job description, there is often little time to understand completely what is happening within the workplace. These dedicated leaders don't know what they don't know, and their employees won't tell them what they don't know, so they remain blissfully—or stressfully—unaware of a major problem until it explodes. In business, as in combat, having the correct information is the key to victory. Hard work is not enough. Dedication is not enough. The Light Horse Brigade had both, and look what happened to them. We can never reach our potential if we fail to have a complete understanding of our strengths and weaknesses. An assessment will provide this information, and one should be conducted in each organization every few years.

I feel strongly that assessment information should be compiled into a detailed document that can be studied before making rash decisions. Also, it takes time to understand the different perceptions that people have about the organization. Leaders who examine the assessment information should remember one foundational truth: Perception is reality. In other words, some of the information contained in the assessment may not be true, but it will be real to the person who contributed it.

For example, I have had foundational level employees say that their managers don't care about them. The employees were convinced that this was true and even supported their assertions with stories of uncaring acts by their leaders. However, subsequent discussions with their managers revealed that they really did care about their employees, but they had never taken the time to communicate or demonstrate it. Therefore, the managers' actions were perceived as uncaring, and the employees reacted accordingly.

FEEDBACK TO EVERYONE

Soon after the information gathered during the assessment has been compiled, it should be communicated back to *everyone* who participated in the interviews. This is contrary to many organizations' practices of conducting opinion surveys without building into the process official feedback to employees. I have found that feedback is essential for building the trust needed for change. Leaders often resist sharing negative information with their followers for fear that the information will demoralize them or show weaknesses in the organization or its leaders. This is faulty thinking for two reasons. First, followers are well aware of the organization's deficiencies and are glad that leaders are finally going to address the problems. Leader openness will be seen as a sign of strength and integrity rather than weakness. Second, commitment from followers is vital, and sharing the assessment results allows them to participate fully in the change process, thus promoting that commitment.

FEEDBACK METHODS AND LESSONS LEARNED

Not only should the information gathered during an assessment be fed back to everyone who participated in the interviews, but also that it should be done in person, not through documents, memos, or bulletins, which are often misinterpreted. Once an assessment or survey has been commissioned, leaders should *always* share the results with followers and allow sufficient time for questions and answers.

There are some simple guidelines to follow during the feedback. Leaders should not promise that all weaknesses can be eliminated within a short period of time. This expectation may be unrealistic. Followers just need to hear that the issues will be dealt with in a reasonable period of time. Also, leaders should not minimize, place blame, or make excuses for any actual shortcomings. Excuses aren't reasons. Excuses don't create positive change. Leaders should be prepared to explain any misunderstandings or misperceptions that the assessment identifies. In my experience, at least 40 percent of the problems identified during an assessment result from misperception, miscommunication, and misunderstanding. These are easily reconciled with proper explanation. This results in an immediate boost in employee morale and bottom-line performance.

A WORD OF CAUTION

Unlike the top manager at the start of this chapter, leadership *must* accept the survey results with an open mind. If the data is critical of the organization or its leadership, resentment is too often the primary reaction of leaders. Leaders must remember that this information is to be used wisely and logically. The employees did not identify organizational problems to hurt anyone's feelings; they did so to help the organization become its best.

My father spent thirty years as a high-level manager in one of America's largest automotive manufacturing companies. His company often conducted surveys to measure progress, performance, and employee opinions. One such survey found fault with the top management of their operation. The survey identified numerous areas for improvement and was critical of the overall lack of direction. My dad and the other executives were amazed, amused, and ultimately disturbed by their top executive's response to the survey. Rather than addressing the deficiencies, the executive angrily announced that the people who had conducted the survey were incompetent, and he said that a new survey would have to be completed. That was the beginning of the end of that manager's credibility.

A proper assessment is designed to focus on future change, not on past blame.

The next survey produced essentially the same results. Predictably, the manager refused to accept it as well . . . and that was the end of his credibility. Remember, the goal of an assessment is to determine what problems exist and how to address them, not to point blame at who initially may have caused the problems. A proper assessment is designed to focus on future change, not on past blame. Approached in this positive manner, organizations now are ready to move forward into a bright future.

THE BLUEPRINT FOR CHANGE

Once an assessment has been completed and accepted by leadership, things begin to get exciting! The assessment has identified the organization's strengths and weaknesses. Even if serious weaknesses in relationships, communication, or other areas are found, leaders are motivated and mobilized because they now know where to focus their energies. The initial reaction from their followers ranges from skepticism to euphoria; finally the truth is known about their organization. This truth sets the minds of employees free. The past begins to lose its hold as a better future calls. Leaders have clarified the mission, core values, priorities, and operating principles. Now the time has come to develop a comprehensive, long-term plan that uses the assessment results as a blueprint for change. This should be a written document that details timelines, budgets, required resources, and other pertinent information.

THE MISSING FACTOR IN MOST STRATEGIC PLANS

Strategic planning should be an integral part of every organization on earth. A wide variety of issues are incorporated into an organization's strategic plan. Organizations spend considerable time planning for success in areas that include information systems, marketing, financial strategies, facility utilization, equipment and supplies, product innovation, quality assurance, profitability, productivity, and many others. Sadly, the human or cultural side of the planning process is often overlooked or viewed as less important than the issues of technology, infrastructure, and equipment. This is tunnel vision of the worst kind. Every part of every strategic plan will impact people in one way or another.

Also, it is the organization's human resources that will cause the strategic plan to succeed or fail. No strategic plan can be considered complete until it addresses the human side of the equation. Many books have been written about strategic planning, and for good reason. The planning process is anything but easy. I recommend that leaders do a lot of research before they develop strategic plans. Strategic planning calls for thoroughness and attention to detail, in addition to innovation. Strategic planning should not be a trial-and-error process, so it makes sense to learn from others who have done it before. Too much is at risk to take the planning phase lightly. This is especially true when planning for a positive culture.

THE COMPONENTS OF CULTURE

Often, organizational assessments show that a company is performing satisfactorily in the technical or noncultural areas, but it has room for improvement in human relationships. Some of the most common cultural problem areas include leadership effectiveness, teamwork, communication, unclear behavioral expectations, customer service, conflict resolution, reconciliation skills, and trust.

Since productive interpersonal relationships are the foundation for positive change, it is necessary to develop a strategic plan for improving relational skills to shape the organization's culture.

CULTURE BY DESIGN OR DEFAULT?

At this point, leaders must ask themselves one simple question: Do we want to develop our organization's culture by design or allow it to "happen" by default? The only rational answer is by design. If these leaders are serious about success, then they must approach cultural development with the same diligence as they approach their marketing, sales, or quality improvement plans.

Once it has been decided that cultural development is something to be pursued, the rest of the process is quite logical. The leaders review their vision, mission, and core value statements to determine what type of culture will best support these stated goals. Then, they design a plan to create the awareness and skills necessary for all employees to contribute to the cultural development process. I have found that the most effective plans are long-term and are designed to include every employee in multiple skill development sessions.

The following are the essential elements of a plan that we recently helped a client develop. This information will give a basic understanding of how to put the cultural components together and how to create realistic timelines for everything that needs to be accomplished.

We began the process by reviewing the company's statements of vision, mission, and values. Every initiative in our cultural development plan had to support one or more of these statements, or it would be eliminated. We then wrote the following statement that explains what the plan is intended to accomplish. Next, we established some guiding principles for the cultural transformation initiative.

STATEMENT OF INTENT

Our cultural development plan is designed to deliver a comprehensive program that includes cultural awareness and alignment, clear behavioral expectations, leadership and staff development, customer service enhancements, process improvement, and effective change management.

GUIDING PRINCIPLES

Cultural Transformation. We intend to focus on the adaptations necessary to maintain an aligned culture and to respond effectively to a changing environment.

Education and Professional Development. We intend to promote competence and character in all leaders and staff, encouraging effective performance and continuous improvement.

Systems and Work Processes. We intend to focus on standards, evaluation, and continuous process improvements, using team problem solving and creativity to promote effective systems.

This information provided the broad framework for our plan. Next, it was time to identify a list of general initiatives needed to create a learning organization. Based on the company's guiding statements and our assessment data, we selected the following initiatives to pursue. Also, this meant that we needed to identify and match specific, measurable education and training activities to each initiative.

Cultural development initiatives

Cultural orientation meetings
New-employee orientation sessions
New manager/supervisor orientation sessions
Internal communications audit and enhancement process
Employee survey and follow-up

Leadership development initiatives

Coaching and mentoring process
Leadership training courses
Team building for executive team and management group
Continuous reinforcement activities

Staff development initiatives

Interpersonal relationships training programs
Team building and targeted intervention where needed
Quality and customer service initiatives
Customer service team and network development
Facilitation and team leader training
Problem-solving and decision-making training
Continuous quality improvement training

Once we identified the major initiatives and specific activities needed to build the culture, all that remained was to create a long-term schedule or calendar of events. This can be very tedious due to the logistics of scheduling large numbers of people to attend various training sessions. However, investing several hours during the initial planning often saves many wasted days later in the process.

The final part of the planning process is to identify which activities will be scheduled first. Typically, we want to begin with leadership development so that the organization's leaders are prepared to model the proper behaviors for their new culture. Once an activity like leadership training has been selected, it is time to decide on the details of what will be taught, when the training sessions will be held, how many sessions will be required, and which leaders will attend first.

To continue the implementation of the cultural development plan, leaders need to identify the activities that logically follow and repeat the scheduling process until the schedule is completed. In the next few chapters, we will explore specific training content and educational topics that can be presented to both leaders and followers.

MOMENTUM FOR CHANGE

Once the strategic plan for cultural development is created, it is pursued in combination with the organization's statement of mission, core values, and operating principles. At this stage, the change initiative is like a giant rock that is beginning to roll downhill. It may have been difficult to move initially, but now it is virtually impossible to stop. The people involved know the organization's purpose and direction, and they also know the strategy of how to accomplish the mission. They are willing, and with the help of education and training outlined in their plan, they will be more than able to make it happen.

QUESTIONS AND REFLECTIONS

Business • Government • Ministry • Family • Personal

1. In your organization, how is everyone kept informed of good news? Bad news?

2. Are surveys, assessments, and questionnaires used to gather information? What happens to the results?

3. Does your organization have a strategic plan for the future? If so, how was the plan developed? Who contributed? Who did not? Does everyone understand the plan?

4. Is there a serious commitment to a strategic plan within your organization?

5. Do you have a strategic plan for your life?

CHAPTER 12

THE ROLE OF EDUCATION AND TRAINING

"You can't teach an old dog new tricks!" smirked the young know-it-all from the back of the conference hall. "Our company should just get rid of all the older employees. Lots of them don't even have college degrees and seem pretty stupid! They don't want to learn anyway."

I had just finished presenting a plan for change to his company's management team and had asked for comments. Big mistake! This junior executive was armed with a new MBA degree, expensive leather suspenders, and lots of theory . . . but he lacked any real-world experience. That is a very dangerous combination. He was challenging my recommendation that all employees be involved in training to help eliminate the adversarial relationships between labor and management. I confess that I have a difficult time remaining civil when confronted with prejudice, so my response to him was pointed.

"First," I said, "I don't know who would appreciate a new trick more than an old dog. Second, each of the older employees represents to your company an investment of approximately one million dollars. It would be very foolish to throw that away. Third, education does not equate to intelligence. The employees whom you are so anxious to discard have had the intelligence to run this place for years without too much involvement from anyone. They literally are in charge of the entire operation on second and third shift, when most managers have gone home for the night."

By this time, the young executive's smirk had transformed into a frown, but at least he was listening to the message.

"Finally," I said, as I tried to regain my own composure, "the whole issue of core values comes into play here. You should remember that these employees are the ones whose hard work and sacrifice over the years have made it possible for you to even have a job. They deserve a chance to learn and enhance their skills the same as you do."

It occurred to me that this zealous young man was a lot like the preacher who was so heavenly minded he was no earthly good. The young executive had never taken time to see if his philosophy made sense in the real world. Fortunately, senior management saw the value of my recommendations and requested the training for all employees. The results were tremendous. Older employees proved the young critic wrong as they not only excelled in the training, but also played an active role in the change effort. The education and training gave everyone in the organization a new mind-set and the corresponding skills to go with it. The organization began to prosper as never before.

The value of educating employees is no secret. During the late 1990s, organizations in the United States alone invested about $65 billion per year in workplace education and training. In 1998, the Gallup Organization released the results of a survey that showed some interesting facts about this subject. The survey showed that 84 percent of employees who received at least six days of training within the previous year said they were satisfied with their jobs, compared to only 70 percent of those who received no job training. Eighty percent of the people surveyed said that the availability of company-sponsored training programs was a factor in deciding whether to accept a new job or remain in their current positions.

Education and training are no longer options for the business world; they have become necessities. Just as no organization can afford to allow its equipment to become obsolete, neither can it allow its human resources to become outdated. As our world continues to change, we must upgrade our people's skills, knowledge, and awareness. In the race for survival, we must use basic education and training to keep pace with competitors. If we wish to advance beyond the pack, then we need to educate employees. We must arm them with new information so that they can generate solutions to problems that don't yet exist.

PREVENTIVE MAINTENANCE FOR RELATIONSHIPS?

Somehow leaders must develop an entirely new mind-set when it comes to workplace education and training. We need a change in the training paradigm similar to the one that occurred in preventive maintenance programs. These programs were instituted in countless organizations that had machines, equipment, and technology capable of breakdown. Some wise person discovered that it made more sense to invest time performing minor repairs, upgrading technology, and maintaining equipment at regular intervals—even when things were running properly—than to mindlessly wait for random breakdowns to occur. Perhaps we should paint employees a neutral color and attach power cords to them. This may help us remember that people's performance and relationships can break down at the worst possible time, leaving a company to flounder. A pilot strike in the late 1990s cost onc airline company more than two hundred million dollars. I wonder whether some preventive maintenance performed on the relationships between management and the pilots *before* the strike would have prevented the sad waste of money, time, and energy.

To achieve this new mind-set, we first must realize that any money spent on employee education is a wise investment rather than just another cost. People are the only resources that have such limitless capacities to think, reason, innovate, solve problems, and plan. An untrained employee is similar to a new computer system that no one has programmed. Each has the capacity to do great things. But since they are not prepared to perform properly, they may be a liability to the organization. I encourage our clients to think of their organizations in terms of a "corporate university." This is where every member of the organization is both a potential student and a teacher.

Organizations will not change until people change!

In this setting, every employee watches for opportunities to learn, grow, and teach new skills to others. With the corporate university concept, people are not satisfied with the status quo; they constantly are looking for ways to expand their knowledge about a wide variety of topics, including products, services, customers, suppliers, markets, and especially their competitors. As members of the corporate university, each employee seeks to learn new ways to do old things. They replace the old adage, "If it ain't broke, don't fix it!" with one of their own: "If it ain't broke, let's see how we can make it better before our competitors do!" Students at our corporate universities include senior citizens, baby boomers, and Generation Xers. They have unique reasons for wanting to participate in workplace education programs and are highly motivated by them. No one wants merely to exist in a job that has no sense of newness. Employees no longer are willing just to go through monotonous motions with no promise of excitement or innovation in their jobs. They want to combine company-sponsored continuing education with their work. The list of courses that benefit employees seems endless. It includes training in technical areas, customer service, computer literacy, supervisory skills, international business, second languages, government regulations, benefit application, and a wide variety of human relations training.

To summarize, change either creates something new or renews something that already exists. Successful change requires people to expand or renew their thinking about their world, their organizations, and themselves. Common sense tells us that to obtain new results, something new must be attempted. A wise person once said, "If you do what you have always done, you will get what you have always got." What the statement lacks in proper grammar, it makes up for in truth. And the truth is, organizations will not change until the people within them change! This seems so obvious, but it is amazing how many managers are frustrated by the lack of positive progress in their organizations and yet fail to teach their employees the basic skills needed to compete with other companies. Often, the people involved want to change, but they don't know how. I have had some really heated discussions with top managers who demanded continuous improvement in their work environment without providing continuing education opportunities for workers. No matter how much leaders threaten, motivate, reward, or scold their employees, they will fail to see continuous improvement in their bottom-line performances without first equipping employees with new information, new skills, or new equipment.

THE GOAL OF EDUCATION AND TRAINING

For many leaders, the greatest challenge of change is transferring their understanding of what must be accomplished and how it will be accomplished to the foundational levels of the organization. Successfully transferring this vital information requires much more than a quick memo or even a company-wide meeting to succeed. It necessitates a systematic education and training process that ensures all members of the company clearly understand and can accomplish the plan. Therefore, the goal of workplace education and training is very basic. It is to equip people with the relevant information, knowledge, and skills necessary for them to be productive. Training must be designed to build support for the change process and enhance employee competence as it progresses.

As I reflect on our assessments of a wide variety of organizations, three areas on the human or cultural side of the equation consistently require education and training. They are leadership, team building or interpersonal relations, and problem solving. These areas represent the foundational skills and principles that organizations must have in place to promote change, growth, and excellence among employees. Leadership training ensures that top-and-middle level managers and supervisors are prepared to initiate the change process. The team-building/interpersonal relations training provides employees with skills necessary to work effectively with others. Finally, problem-solving training empowers people with skills to address problems, make decisions, and develop effective plans as they press toward the mission. The next three chapters will provide more details on each of these training topics.

WE MUST GET BELOW THE SURFACE

In today's world, education and training need to go beyond basic skill development or skill reinforcement. Effective training not only must impart new skills into the learners' minds, but also touch their hearts. For example, one common problem in the corporate world today relates to *communication*—at least, many problems are categorized that way. Countless training sessions are designed each year to teach people the basic skills and techniques of communicating with others. Unfortunately, many of these sessions are a complete waste of time and money. Attendees file into classrooms, listen to instructors, practice how to organize their thoughts, and speak clearly to their coworkers. At the end of the training session, they march back to their workstations and discover that their communication is no more effective than before the session. Why? Because often, the real problem with corporate communications is not that people don't know how to communicate; rather, they choose not to communicate. The solution here deals more with impacting *wills* than upgrading skills. Also, too many people simply don't understand how to develop and maintain the healthy relationships required for effective communication in the work environment. They often are incredibly insensitive about the impact of their words on others.

I recall a warehouse manager who was having a terrible time with employee morale and productivity. Although I spent several days interviewing his entire workforce, I knew what caused his problems by the end of the first day of assessment. I learned that this manager had attended what I call a "one-day-wonder" training session where he learned "all that he needed to learn about management"—or so said the flyer he received in the mail—in less than eight hours. Despite the fact that thousands of people attend these sessions each year, I still consider them to be a lot like the dainty finger foods served as appetizers at cocktail parties. They look appealing, but they always leave you hungry for a real meal.

At any rate, this manager left the training session with just enough understanding of several concepts to be dangerous to his employees' morale, his organization's success, and his own career. It seems that he had learned a new term called *value added* while at the seminar. From that day on, he felt compelled to include the concept whenever he addressed his employees. Unfortunately, his message came across in the worst possible way. He literally told his employees that warehousing was a nonvalue-adding function of the manufacturing process, and therefore, the employees' efforts did not add value to their corporation. Naturally, the employees were hurt, angry, and demotivated by his insensitive and inaccurate comments. His problem was not one of basic communication. Believe me, his employees understood exactly what he was saying. Instead, his problem was that he failed to anticipate *how* his message would impact his audience.

To be clear, I favor teaching communication skills. My company has done so for years. However, I have learned that we first must teach people how communication impacts their relationships with others before we teach new techniques of speaking and listening. Training must prick the conscience of those who choose not to treat others with respect, kindness, and common courtesy if we truly are to improve communications within any work environment.

THE ORDER OF EDUCATION AND TRAINING

For maximum effectiveness, training should be given in the proper order. That is, it should begin at the upper levels of the organization and progress downward. It is important for leaders to participate in any and all training programs that result from an assessment. It is also important that they attend the training *before* their followers. This empowers the leaders with firsthand information about the training and also shows their commitment to the change process.

I recall a large church whose leaders invited us to assist them with staff development. They had significant division among staff members, which was beginning to hinder the church's effectiveness. We designed a series of weekend workshops for them based on what they said they needed.

Key leaders always must be active in the training process!

On the first morning, we were pleased to have the senior pastor address the group and speak of the importance of the training—so far, so good. He then made an announcement that sealed the fate of that group. He said he had decided that he did not need the training and would be leaving to attend to some "important matters." As he left the room, so did any hope of unifying his staff. Their attitudes changed from interested to surly, and the workshop became a test of endurance. Key leaders always must be active in the training process! Once top people have been trained, the rest of the organization follows in order. Often middle-level managers benefit greatly from training in leadership and interpersonal relations. Why? Because while top leaders design and communicate the mission, middle managers actually bring the vision to pass by their daily actions. It is much easier to create a vision than to achieve it. Middle managers and first-line supervisors are usually pleased to receive any high-quality training that helps them succeed in implementing the vision.

Once those in positions of authority have received the training, then it is time to include the remainder of the organization. My experience has proven that foundational-level employees excel in training sessions that are developed out of the original organizational assessment. I have witnessed the incredible transformation that occurs when lower-level employees are given the opportunity to learn new skills. They develop a sense of pride in having mastered new information and eagerly apply it on the job, as well as in their personal lives.

THE PROPER APPROACH TO EDUCATION, TRAINING, AND DEVELOPMENT

Clearly, education and training are integral parts of any change process, since there is a need to continually upgrade both technical and human relations skills; but not all training sessions are successful. I have found that the most effective training programs share three common traits. First, the training must be part of a long-term approach to change, not a quick fix that is soon forgotten. I do not believe in a training blitz in which everyone in an organization is rushed through a few seminars and sent back into an unchanged work environment. It is much better to have individuals attend no more than three days of relevant training at a time, then practice what was learned for several weeks before attending another session.

The second common trait is that the training is practical, rather than theoretical. Obviously, all practical information has its origin in theory. However, trainees should not have to sit through hours of lecture on the theory of relationships, leadership, or anything else for that matter. Instead, they should be given a brief introduction to a topic and then moved quickly into practical lessons that address real organizational problems related to the given topic. The subject matter should always be aligned with needs that were identified during the original organizational assessment or subsequent surveys.

The final characteristic shared by the most effective programs is that the training should be highly participative, rather than lecture-based. Adults interested in positive change tend to be people of action who readily respond to an opportunity to interact with their peers. Education and training built upon short teachings, simulations, small-group discussions, and team projects will capture the attention of participants and ensure that maximum learning will take place.

The need for higher quality training and education will only increase in the future. The reason? Because technology, equipment, regulations, roles, and relationships are constantly doing two things: changing and increasing in complexity. This requires that people be properly trained to succeed in this new work environment. Training takes a serious investment of time, money, and other resources, but there is simply no other way to ensure maximum competitiveness. Remember that the primary complaint of management in the late 1990s was not about the lack of potential employees. Rather, it was about the lack of qualified or properly trained employees. Despite this fact, many leaders today still will gladly spend millions of dollars on new technology, but they balk at spending anything on employee training and development.

Several years ago, I spoke with a business owner who is a classic example of this mind-set. He boasted about the thousands of dollars he had spent on a new computer system that would revolutionize his small manufacturing operation. Every aspect of his company would be computerized, including ordering, manufacturing, accounting, inventory control, and so on. His vision for change was a good one, since up to that point record keeping was inconsistent at best. Inventory counts often were kept on small scraps of paper, and manufacturing runs were based on the supervisor's "gut feel" rather than actual data. The owner's plan for progress broke down, however, when he decided to provide his employees with only a single day of training on the new system. One day! It takes longer than that to learn how to play some computerized video games.

The result of his folly was predictable. His employees gave it their best efforts, but after several months of frustration and pitiful work performance, they began to bypass the computer system to get some work done. Once again, inventory counts were done on napkins, and supervisors used gut feelings as their guides for production runs. Clearly, for peak performance, we need to upgrade both our technical and interpersonal capabilities. However, one of the safest places to invest time and money is in an organization's human resources. Humans may show some signs of wear and tear with age, but we will never become obsolete.

QUESTIONS AND REFLECTIONS

Business • Government • Ministry • Family • Personal

1. Do you have a "corporate university" on your organization's campus? What priority does your organization place on education and training? How is it shown?

2. Do all of the members of your organization have the skills and knowledge necessary for peak performance?

3. In what way is education and training part of your organization's overall strategic plan?

4. How is education and training in your organization practical and applicable to daily performance requirements?

5. What areas in your personal life could be enhanced with some additional education and training?

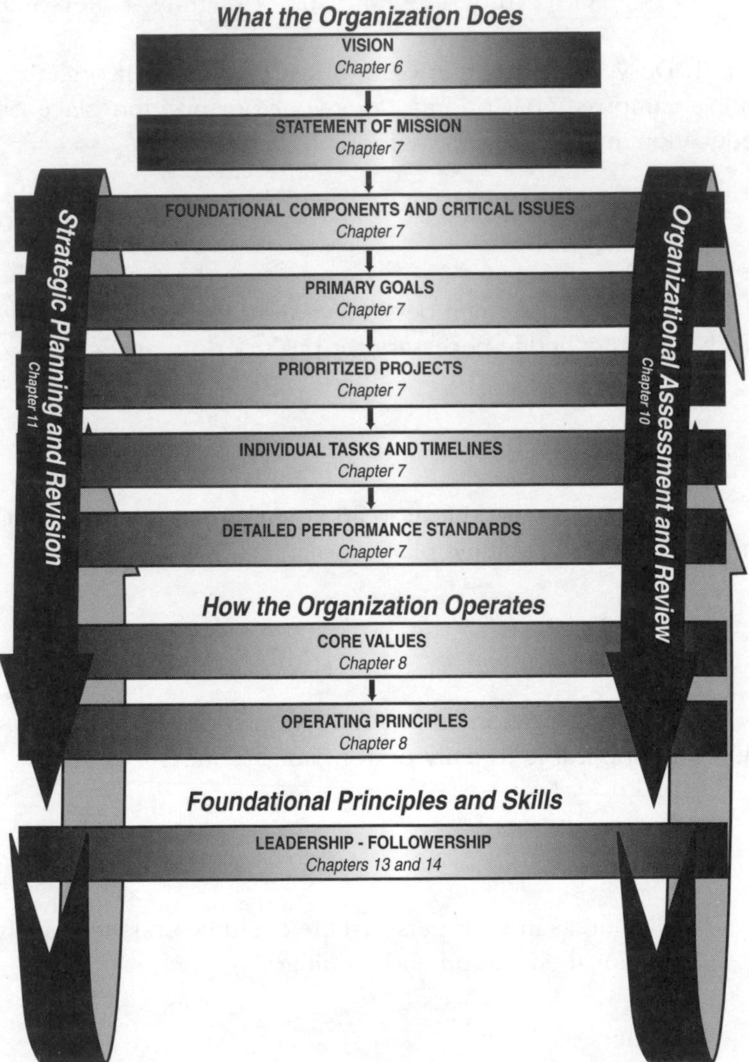
THE MOLITOR DEVELOPMENTAL PROCESS
What the Organization Does
VISION
Chapter 6
STATEMENT OF MISSION
Chapter 7
FOUNDATIONAL COMPONENTS AND CRITICAL ISSUES
Chapter 7
PRIMARY GOALS
Chapter 7
PRIORITIZED PROJECTS
Chapter 7
INDIVIDUAL TASKS AND TIMELINES
Chapter 7
DETAILED PERFORMANCE STANDARDS
Chapter 7
How the Organization Operates
CORE VALUES
Chapter 8
OPERATING PRINCIPLES
Chapter 8
Foundational Principles and Skills
LEADERSHIP - FOLLOWERSHIP
Chapters 13 and 14
Strategic Planning and Revision
Chapter 11
Organizational Assessment and Review
Chapter 10

CHAPTER 13

LEADERSHIP DEVELOPMENT

ATTENTION: Starting Monday morning, employees are not allowed to work together when loading trucks.

SIGNED: The Management.

This sign appeared one morning on the employee bulletin board at a company that sells building supplies. At first, the employees thought that it might be a prank, but close inspection of the sign confirmed that it was an official policy change. Two young managers—who nearly put their family-owned company out of business—had placed it there. I became aware of the sign, its origin, and the turmoil that it caused among workers during an organizational assessment that I had been asked to complete for the company. I discovered that these fledgling leaders were sons of the company owners. Although they each were in their mid-twenties and had been given no formal training, they had been asked to supervise experienced employees, many of whom were more than twice their ages.

Senior laborers told me during our interviews that their new managers initially were tolerated because of employees' commitment to the company owners, who historically had been good men to work for. However, the trouble started when the novices observed two employees laughing as they loaded unwieldy building materials onto a flatbed trailer. Laughing—imagine that! Despite the fact that the work was accomplished well, these young "leaders" decided that employees were having too much fun working together. So they instituted a policy that, from that day on, each employee would load the trailers alone. The employees were furious about this decision, and responded with what I call "malicious" obedience. In other words, they followed the new guidelines even though they knew it would be bad for the company.

As weeks passed, the inevitable began to happen. The work pace slowed dramatically, causing productivity to fall. The cost of damaged goods skyrocketed since much of the material required two men to stabilize during the loading process. Some lost-time injuries occurred as employees strained their backs trying to muscle unwieldy items onto trucks. Naturally, these events caused the young managers to respond in an all-too-typical fashion. They held company-wide meetings to talk to employees about the need for them to do better work. Workers were forced to watch generic safety videotapes and listen to lectures on the importance of productivity. At times, the frustrated managers even scolded employees for not working smart enough. On at least one occasion, the word *lazy* was mentioned. Employee morale plummeted to its lowest level in company history.

Amazingly, the top managers of the company were not aware that the policy had been instituted until the assessment revealed it as a source of employee dissatisfaction. Eventually, top management forced the embarrassed young managers to change the unproductive policy, but much was lost in the interim. The unrestricted reign of the novices had compromised productivity, morale, customer satisfaction, safety, management credibility, and workplace unity. One bad leadership decision caused all of this trouble.

I don't place the blame for this fiasco solely on the young managers. Following the initial assessment, I spent time coaching both of them, and our discussions confirmed my suspicions. Their own leaders had thrust them into their positions with little preparation. The only coaching that senior managers had given them had come in the form of cryptic sound bytes. Statements such as, "Show 'em who's boss!" and "Give 'em an inch and they'll take a mile!" shaped the thinking of these young men. Because of these teachings, this dangerous duo viewed the foundation of leadership as maintaining strict control over the workplace. No wonder they saw employee laughter as the first stage of an impending rebellion.

Could this negative situation have been avoided? Of course! Imagine the difference if top management had talked with these young men about some foundations of leadership before they made the policy change.

Senior manager: "Look at Bill and Jim over on the loading dock. Man, they sure know how to load delivery trucks. Our customers never complain. Those guys are the best! They have a good time at work, too. I love to hear them laugh. You know why? It means they are happy. Isn't that great?"

These words are all it would have taken for the young men to begin the transformation from immature power mongers to effective leaders.

LEADING THE FOLLOWERS

I am convinced that the people who must change first in any organization are the leaders. Whether young or old, they provide the model for all others to follow. Therefore, the higher the position of leadership that a person has, the more crucial it is for him to be visibly supportive of the direction and culture of the organization. This is especially true during periods of uncertainty or when a change process is underway. Presidents, plant managers, and parents are the ones who will cause the process to succeed or fail in the initial stages. People in key positions of leadership need to be positive role models for others to follow. This creates an interesting challenge for top leaders who have spent years using less-than-positive methods to attain their current positions. During their rise to position, power, and influence, they developed habitual patterns in their approaches to leadership.

Some of these patterns are good, others are not. For example, one leader may have risen to success by finding ways to hurt the careers of rivals within the organization. Another may have learned that the best way to lead was to embarrass and belittle other workers. Still another has found that if he tells small lies to acquire new customer accounts, his performance can surpass that of his peers. Too many managers and supervisors use a command-and-control style of leadership that would be appropriate for hardened veterans in combat, but it is hardly suitable in today's workplace. While any of these approaches to leadership may have worked in the past, they certainly will cause problems in a modern work environment. For example, a command-and-control type of leader may succeed in a relatively stable business environment where the performance of followers can be closely monitored. However, this type of leader is ill equipped when conditions become more challenging and the follower's complete commitment is needed for the organization to prosper. Also, a person who has gained promotion by using ruthless tactics finds that he is not trusted by anyone, especially in a rapidly changing environment. This lack of trust will slow his ability to produce, ultimately resulting in discredit to the leader.

I see leadership more as an art than a science. It is much more than a set of simple techniques or strategies to get others to perform. Leadership is a complex combination of attitudes, behaviors, standards, and communication patterns that are applied consistently with a maximum amount of concern for followers. Therefore, leaders continually must evaluate and enhance their effectiveness or risk losing followers' support.

THE HEART OF THE MATTER

With all that is written and said about leadership these days, it may be difficult for managers and supervisors to decide what their top priorities should be. I am convinced that the most crucial area for a leader to focus on is his or her heart. I am not referring to the blood-pumping organ that resides in our chest cavities. I'm talking about the very core of a person's nature. Leaders must care about others and, therefore, act in a manner that proves their concern. This element is missing in too many discussions and teachings about leadership.

At some point in every leadership seminar and workshop that I teach, I ask attendees one simple question about themselves as leaders. Do they care about their followers? I force them to consider whether they view the people they lead as living, breathing human beings, or as something less than that, perhaps no more than as names or numbers on a report sheet. The room usually gets quiet as people ponder their responses. Leadership begins and ends in the heart. No techniques can motivate followers when they know their leaders don't care about them. Conversely, there is no end to what followers will attempt for leaders who have shown that they truly care. This is the heart of the matter. This is the foundation for leadership that will last.

LEADERSHIP DEVELOPMENT

Leadership is more than management or supervision. Leadership deals with a person's ability to influence, motivate, and guide others in the accomplishment of a mission. Much of the teaching and instruction that people receive in preparation for leadership focuses on managing projects, materials, sales, and finances, but fails to prepare them to actually lead people. Our world is filled with individuals who can manage the status quo, but there is a shortage of people who can rally others around a new vision. Fortunately, the leadership skills needed today are those that can be learned; therefore, we simply need to develop those skills in our current executives, managers, supervisors, pastors, and parents.

A PROCESS WITHIN A PROCESS

There are two approaches that we can use to secure effective leaders for our organizations. Only one makes any sense in the real world. The first approach is to assign a committee the task of searching the world to locate the best of the best to fill our leadership positions. They would need to find people with natural leadership abilities, charisma, intuitive insights into all aspects of life, integrity, caring, and an intense commitment to the organization's vision. Naturally, people possessing these qualities will have nothing better to do than wait for the organization to call with a job offer.

As long as we are dreaming, let's find people who would willingly accept employment at a very low level of compensation. Once hired, these individuals would bond instantly with all followers, create innovative methods of production, secure new and lucrative contracts and, during their break, galvanize relationships with their coleaders. Does this sound too good to be true? It is. The basic problem with this fantasy is that perfect leaders simply cannot be found. No human beings are born with all of the qualities we want in our leaders. We all enter this world with a wonderful combination of God-given gifts and talents. However, by the time we enter the workforce, we also have developed a full range of misconceptions, prejudices, weaknesses, and bad habits. In other words, if your strategy for leadership is to hire only perfect candidates, you will be disappointed. It simply is not going to happen.

The opposite approach is just as bad. It is amazing that so many organizations hire people, put them in leadership positions, and hope for the best. That is a very dangerous strategy, or, more accurately, *lack* of strategy. The second—and obviously better—approach is this: We begin by hiring the best candidates available. With proper screening, we select candidates who, through education and previous work experiences, have demonstrated at least some of the attributes we want in our leaders. Then, we make no assumptions about their capabilities or their understanding of our organization's expectations for leadership performance. We sit with each new leader and clearly explain our vision, mission, and core values. We then explain how his or her role as a leader is vital to accomplishing the mission. Next, we assess the strengths and weaknesses of the new leader and design a developmental process to enhance his or her skills. This entire process is built upon the foundation of clear leadership expectations.

LEADERSHIP EXPECTATIONS

The first step in the process of leadership development is to clarify the organization's expectations for leadership behavior. This is accomplished by writing a list of essential attitudes, behaviors, and activities that are desired in leaders. Failure to do so would be similar to asking a marksman to shoot a bull's-eye without first providing a target. They may use up a lot of ammunition and make a lot of noise, but they never really succeed.

The primary source of leadership expectations is found in an organization's statements of vision, mission, and core values.

This is why it is so important that each organization completes, *in sequence,* each step of the development process covered in this book. Each step builds on the previous step and prepares for the following step. Therefore, if you skip one step, you will have major problems later in the process.

Leadership expectations should be in writing and may be recorded in a number of different ways. These include individual bullet points, a series of sentences describing the desired behavior, or a more comprehensive paragraph that contains a complete description of expectations.

One of our recent clients chose to record expectations for leaders in the following manner. First, they selected the five broad categories of expectations for their leaders: strategic thinking, character, interpersonal skills, job performance, and results. Then, they wrote a paragraph for each characteristic that explained how it could be demonstrated in the work environment. For example, they wrote the following about their first characteristic, strategic thinking. *Strategic thinking signifies the ability to be creative in exciting a work group toward a target or goal. A strategic leader uses current knowledge and skills and is able to think outside of current practices, roles, and conditions to create new solutions.*

Similar paragraphs were written for the four remaining characteristics.

Once leadership expectations are clarified and recorded, they are shared with all leaders. This creates a work environment in which each leader has a common understanding of how these behaviors will help accomplish their mission and shape the organization's culture. Next, the organization must evaluate the current level of leadership effectiveness of all executives, managers, and supervisors.

The following steps outline the leadership enhancement process.

INITIAL EVALUATION, MEASUREMENT, AND FEEDBACK

This information often comes from organizational assessment results. It is common for an assessment to identify leadership practices that need improvement and even where the most serious deficiencies exist. This information also can be gathered from focus groups and written employee opinion surveys.

EDUCATION AND TRAINING

Often, leaders perform poorly because they have never been taught a better way to lead. Many managers, supervisors, government officials, and clergy have never learned anything other than what their own leaders previously taught them. If they were fortunate enough to serve under leaders who taught them to care for and respect their followers, then they will probably succeed in today's world. If, however, they suffered under a command-and-control or otherwise unprincipled leader, they will need education and training in new methods of leadership.

LEADERSHIP COACHING AND MENTORING

To a casual observer, leadership must seem a lot like playing golf: Both look easy. Just stand up and hit the ball, right? Just stand up and motivate a group of people to accomplish a mission, right? Wrong! Both are much more difficult than they appear. Every novice who tries the game of golf soon learns the value of instruction from an experienced golfer. Coaching often means the difference between success and failure. A good coach points out the subtleties of the game that separate average golfers from great ones.

So it is with leadership. We all can use some help perfecting our leadership "swing." Often, we aren't even aware of our mistakes, so we continue to practice leading others improperly. Unfortunately, the longer we practice something incorrectly, the harder it is to change because we first must unlearn our mistakes before we can learn the proper way. This is why changing a senior manager's or longtime supervisor's approach to leadership is a challenge. They often struggle to unlearn certain unproductive practices.

At the other end of the training spectrum, there is a special need for skill development in young leaders. No one can do more harm or good than a relatively new supervisor, manager, or parent. Unless zeal is tempered by education, training, coaching, and counseling, these people may endanger the mission and cause harm to followers. On the bright side, once a young person receives proper instruction in leadership, he can spend a lifetime successfully leading others.

Through the years, I have learned that it is important for all leaders to receive some unbiased coaching and mentoring during their careers. In the corporate world, it is very common for a leader's performance to be evaluated only by one person above him in the organization. This is a dangerous way to determine the effectiveness of any leader. Why? Because an executive or manager can evaluate a subordinate leader's ability to follow directions or accomplish a given set of tasks, but may have difficulty evaluating that person's ability to lead others. This top-down evaluation can create organizational blind spots that are very damaging to everyone involved. A better approach is to obtain feedback on a person's performance from that person's leaders, peers, and subordinates. Several years ago, I designed a personalized leadership coaching process to give people this type of 360-degree feedback. The original intent of this process, which we call EXECUTIVE *A PLUS,* was to help marginally effective leaders improve their performance; however, that soon changed.

The EXECUTIVE *A PLUS* process is simple, but it works. We have the leader, his supervisors, peers, followers, and, in some rare cases, family members complete a confidential written survey of the person's leadership strengths and weaknesses. Then, we compile the survey information into a written report that provides numerical ratings and extensive comments about the leader. Next, we select one of our staff to serve as a personal coach or mentor to feed back the information to the leader and help him set performance improvement goals.

Once the goals are set, the coach has weekly mentoring sessions with the leader to help fine-tune his performance and ensure commitment to the goals. The relationship between coach and leader is a very special one. Trust and confidentiality typify their interactions. The role of coach is one of listening and helping the leader identify hidden keys to improve his current performance. This process continues for approximately four months, and then the leader is reevaluated.

Our initial results were very good using the EXECUTIVE *A PLUS* process. The reevaluations showed that over 70 percent of the marginal leaders made significant improvement in their leadership effectiveness as a result of the coaching. As these marginal performers became more effective on their jobs, an amazing thing happened. Some of the very best leaders in the same organizations asked to participate in the EXECUTIVE *A PLUS* process. Unlike the first group of leaders who needed to improve their performances or possibly lose their jobs, these top performers wanted to raise their leadership effectiveness to the next level. Invariably, even these top leaders found one or two areas for improvement. Often, they had blind spots that were exposed by the honest feedback. Amazingly the results were even better with this type of leader, with well over 90 percent of them experiencing significant gains in performance! I am convinced that training, by itself, is not enough to help most leaders attain peak performance. Coaching and mentoring are vital components in the process of leadership enhancement and should become part of every organization's developmental process.

ONGOING EVALUATION OF PERFORMANCE AND FEEDBACK

I have heard it said that we must inspect what we expect. In other words, it is not enough to set expectations, provide training, and then coach our leaders. We also must provide each leader with regular feedback on performance. The purpose of this process is not to catch a leader doing something wrong. On the contrary, it is to help leaders improve if they are slipping in some area of leadership and, more importantly, to catch them doing something *right*. Leaders need consistent encouragement, and should be rewarded for doing a good job. If we fail to evaluate performance, we will not know how to assist leaders in their personal pursuit of excellence. Again, this assessment may come from formal surveys or informal evaluation methods specific to an organization.

KEY PRINCIPLES OF LEADERSHIP

Our research has revealed some fascinating things about what followers look for in their leaders. Contrary to popular belief, successful leaders don't need to be flamboyant, witty, charismatic, or ruthless. We have interviewed literally thousands of followers who identify a very different set of qualities that they admire in their leaders. Ideal leaders consistently demonstrate excellence in four foundational areas. These areas follow and are in no specific order.

CLEAR PURPOSE AND DIRECTION

Leaders must demonstrate that they know where they want their organizations to go and how to get there. Therefore, leaders need to be familiar with the directional concepts of vision, mission, goals, and priorities. Followers always watch how their leaders use resources and if the proper people are placed in positions of authority to accomplish the mission. They also watch to see if top management is committed to a constant purpose and a consistent direction.

Legendary football coach Tom Landry once said that a leader's job was to make people do what they never wanted to do, so that they could become what they always wanted to become. At the start of each season, his players knew that their ultimate reason to exist was to play in the Super Bowl and win the championship. Therefore, they prepared with this in mind from the first day of practice. The result? They became one of the most successful teams in the history of the National Football League.

CARING

Followers never give full commitment to a leader who does not truly care for them. The world is full of self-serving power holders, who are easily identified by even the newest follower. Therefore, one of the most powerful attributes that leaders can exhibit is that they care. Caring is a quality that sets great leaders above good ones. However, caring is often overlooked by many in positions of authority. This is especially true where a leader's performance is measured solely by achievement of short-term financial or operational objectives. Obviously, leaders whose performance reviews do not include evaluation of human relations may look at the quality of caring for employees as unnecessary. This shortsighted approach to leadership overlooks one simple fact: Leadership is *all* about human relations. We can manage processes. We can supervise projects. But we must lead our people.

The common denominator for every business, government, educational institution, and family is people. We must remember that a follower's commitment, sacrifice, and ultimate performance is directly linked to his perception of how much the organization's leaders care for him. Is this an exaggeration? Hardly. Consider how you respond to a lack of caring from a waiter, doctor, or supervisor.

I recently made plans to take my wife to a special restaurant for dinner on our anniversary. I called several days ahead to make reservations, and I explained to the manager that we wanted to be seated in a quiet booth in the back of the dining area. The manager assured me that he would have our booth ready when we arrived. So far, so good.

We anticipated an excellent experience as we drove to the restaurant. When we arrived, the hostess led us into the dining area. The first hint of a problem came when I noticed that all of the booths were filled. To my surprise, the hostess took us to the most crowded area of the restaurant to seat us. I mentioned our anniversary, the reservations, and the promise of a private booth, but to no avail. She responded with a blank look and showed an incredible grasp of the situation when she responded: "Yeah, but the booths are full." I could only shake my head in amazement as my wife and I reluctantly sat down.

Our tiny table looked like an airline tray table that someone had forgotten to lock in its "full and upright position." To make matters worse, the other small tables next to ours were filled with individual diners. The table closest to ours was no more than twelve inches away, and it came complete with a heavyset chain smoker who grunted a greeting to us as we sat down directly across from him.

My plans of an intimate anniversary dinner spent gazing into the eyes of my lovely wife were rapidly disintegrating, so I called the hostess back to check our options. She was even less helpful this time. She mindlessly responded that there was nothing she could do, then pivoted and walked away—no apology, no empathy, nothing. By that time, I was furious at both the incompetence and lack of concern for my wife and me. We unceremoniously left the restaurant and have not been back since.

The same lack of caring that we experienced has caused the downfall of countless businesses, ministries, and personal relationships. Invariably, when we have choices, we avoid uncaring people. If we are forced to interact with them in a work environment, the relationship will be extremely unproductive. Successful leaders today demonstrate strong commitments to both the mission *and* their followers' well-being. People perform beyond their known limitations to satisfy a caring leader.

INTEGRITY

The leader who demonstrates high standards of professional and personal conduct has a tremendous edge over one who is undisciplined or lacking in character. Followers want the assurance that their leaders won't compromise the mission due to a lack of self-control. I have learned that organizations reflect the character of their leaders.

Several years ago, I was consulting with a unionized company where this became evident. The company was attempting to make positive change in its customer service and employee relations. However, members of the local union stubbornly resisted every innovative approach that management tried. Union members even fought against proposed changes that clearly would have benefited them. They threatened management with grievances, complained, and harassed fellow employees who suggested that they try something new. When I questioned some of the employees about their actions, they were evasive and responded with half-truths. This was puzzling, since I believed that they were essentially good people who wanted to do a good job.

The mystery of their negative behavior was solved during their labor-management negotiations. We had been hired to design and facilitate a unique process to resolve their differences with a minimum amount of disruption to their operation. This involved an innovative process that eliminates many of the negative aspects of traditional negotiations. Essentially, the negotiations were to be conducted on a win-win basis, where each side would work to help the other achieve its goals, if at all possible.

On the first day of negotiations, I met the union's local representative. He entered the room fifteen minutes late without smiling and "greeted" us with nothing more than a nod. His behavior got progressively worse as the three-week process wore on. He tried to intimidate everyone, including his own union counterparts. He used the foulest language, even though the lead negotiator for management was a woman. He misrepresented facts, asked for more than what the employees actually needed, and threatened to walk out of the meeting whenever someone disagreed with him.

Communication is the lifeblood of any organization and must be kept flowing to keep its members healthy.

His crowning moment came on the fifth day of the process when he recommended that management deliberately lie to its insurance carrier about some critical aspects of their policy. This proposal could have resulted in a more comprehensive health insurance package for employees but would have jeopardized the credibility of the organization if management had agreed to it. Management quickly declined to be involved with his scheme and moved the discussion to a new topic.

What happened next was amazing and revealed the origin of the employee problem behavior at the company. Less than ten minutes after he had encouraged the company to lie and cheat, the union representative was making a speech about the integrity of his union. In grandiose terms, he explained that management should honor his requests for more money, better health care, and improved working conditions since he would never ask for more than what was absolutely necessary for employees to survive. Even the members of his own committee were visibly embarrassed by this hypocrisy. They later confided in me that this man acted the same way in the monthly union meetings with other members of the workforce. Clearly, his negative attitude and behavior were reflected in the actions of many of the employees on the job. The contract was eventually ratified, but the union leadership lost a great deal of credibility in the process. Integrity is a foundational block in the wall of leadership.

COMMUNICATION AND LISTENING SKILLS

Communication is the lifeblood of any organization and must be kept flowing to keep its members healthy. Therefore, followers need to have a constant stream of clear communication if they are to be effective. They also need to know that those in authority will listen to their suggestions and concerns. Our research has shown that most problems in organizations are caused or magnified by ineffective communication and a lack of listening. Leaders must enhance their abilities in these skill areas or condemn parts of their organizations to failure. There are many methods to enhance communication and listening skills in leaders. Again, education, training, and coaching are the fundamental ways to improve these areas.

One of the highlights of our communication seminars is the material on listening traps. This pleasantly painful exercise is designed to expose our universal inability to listen effectively to others. Instead of listening, we tend to interrupt, contradict, or finish others' sentences. Also, we are preoccupied with everything except the person who is trying to communicate with us. Fortunately, listening is a skill, and once leaders understand its importance, especially during times of change, they can learn to be excellent listeners. Communication and listening are two vitally important keys in opening the hearts of followers and maintaining their commitment to the change process.

THE RESULT OF INCREASED LEADERSHIP EFFECTIVENESS

The importance of leaders operating at peak performance cannot be overstated. Remember that leaders must motivate, encourage, correct, and guide every other person in the organization during the change process. Virtually everything that leaders do and say will be analyzed by followers to see if it supports the vision, mission, core values, and operating principles of the organization. The smallest course variation will be seen as a lack of leaders' commitment to change. If the lack of commitment is perceived to be widespread among leadership, it sentences the change process to a painful death.

As leaders, we should be grateful for the concepts of continuous learning and continuous improvement, and also for external competition. Without these concepts, we easily could become satisfied with the status quo, set in our ways, and ultimately lose our effectiveness. If we are willing, we can learn to be better leaders every day. Even the "old dogs" can learn new tricks from education, training, and counseling from others. Once learned, these new tricks begin a wonderful chain reaction. The proper education and training result in increased leadership effectiveness. Increased leadership effectiveness causes an increase in trust, loyalty, and commitment from followers. It also produces willingness in followers to learn about and change their own attitudes, behaviors, and work performance. The result is both certain and satisfying—mission accomplished!

QUESTIONS AND REFLECTIONS

Business • Government • Ministry • Family • Personal

1. Do leaders of your organization demonstrate the principle of clear purpose and direction? How?

2. How is the principle of caring demonstrated by leaders of your organization?

3. How is the principle of integrity demonstrated by leaders of your organization?

4. How is the principle of communication/listening demonstrated by leaders of your organization?

5. How would your organization change if these principles were demonstrated more?

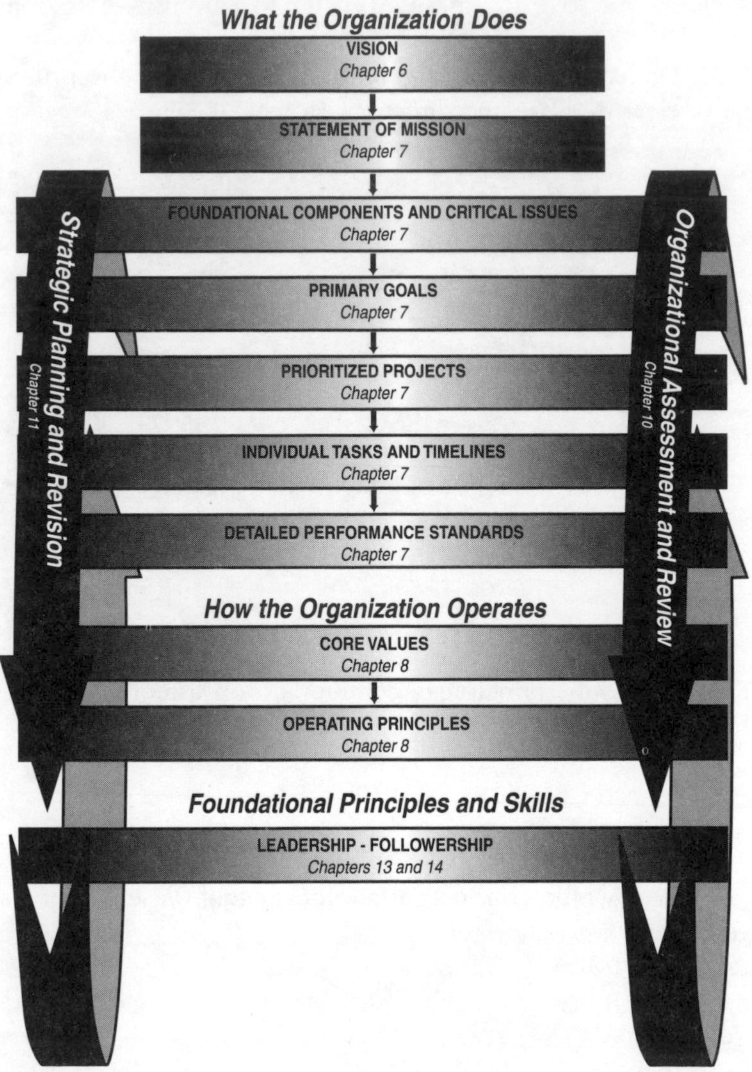
THE MOLITOR DEVELOPMENTAL PROCESS
What the Organization Does
VISION
Chapter 6
STATEMENT OF MISSION
Chapter 7
FOUNDATIONAL COMPONENTS AND CRITICAL ISSUES
Chapter 7
PRIMARY GOALS
Chapter 7
PRIORITIZED PROJECTS
Chapter 7
INDIVIDUAL TASKS AND TIMELINES
Chapter 7
DETAILED PERFORMANCE STANDARDS
Chapter 7
How the Organization Operates
CORE VALUES
Chapter 8
OPERATING PRINCIPLES
Chapter 8
Foundational Principles and Skills
LEADERSHIP - FOLLOWERSHIP
Chapters 13 and 14
Strategic Planning and Revision
Chapter 11
Organizational Assessment and Review
Chapter 10

CHAPTER 14

FOLLOWERSHIP DEVELOPMENT

One of the benefits of living in Michigan is observing the southern migration of Canada geese each fall. Near my home, literally thousands of these magnificent birds stop to feed and rest before continuing their journey. Their approach to the long and difficult trip speaks volumes about leadership and followership. Perhaps they were created as a model for us to copy.

Here is how it works. The birds have clearly identified leaders to guide the flock. Usually, the initial leader is an older bird that has made the journey before. When the leader decides it is time to depart, it heads off in the right direction. Good start! The others form a *V* in flight by aligning themselves on both sides of the leader. Each bird arranges itself immediately behind and slightly to one side of the one ahead of it. In this formation, each bird uses the efforts of the one ahead to minimize the force of the wind pushing against it. This saves a tremendous amount of energy over the duration of the long trip.

As the lead bird sets the course, it takes the brunt of the cruel wind. Eventually, the lead bird gets tired, and an amazing thing occurs. The leader drops back to one end of the *V* formation, where it can rest in flight, literally pulled along by the efforts of geese that had been following it. At the front of the formation, the next bird in line moves into the lead position and follows the course set by the initial leader. At this point, a follower has become the leader. This process of shared responsibility, teamwork, and leading and following continues until the flock reaches the end of its journey. Using this approach, the geese have accomplished their mission with a minimum of effort, protected their leaders from failure, and made provision for the safety of future generations by preparing young followers for leadership. This sounds like a formula for success in any organization. With a little effort, perhaps humans can do as well as these birds.

WHAT'S IN A NAME?

It takes some people a while to get comfortable with the terms *follower* and *followership*. This is caused by a natural tendency for us to want—or at least think we want—to remain independent from other people.

In reality, we are all followers in this life. We follow the instructions, directions, and, in some cases, commands of others as part of our daily routines.

Our bosses, government officials, and public safety officers all provide leadership that we follow. We follow the laws of our nation, state, and community. Traffic signals and directional signs "tell" us what to do and where to go. Deadlines and timelines "lead" us to accomplish tasks. Biblical truths, if we follow them, lead us into proper patterns for life.

In the context of this book, the term *follower* describes someone who looks to someone else for direction as they pursue a common mission. A follower is not a mindless, robot-like person that blindly submits to another's commands. Every organization needs both leaders and followers to succeed. Each has a different role, but they should be seen as having equal value.

FOLLOWING THE LEADERS

When leaders are prepared to operate at peak performance, many wonderful changes occur in their organizations. As leaders show positive attitudes and behaviors, they become role models for followers, who in turn begin to change for the better. Commitment levels rise, and adversarial relationships disappear as followers become part of the change process. This is crucial. Leaders cannot achieve the mission without their followers' help and support. Managers, supervisors, and employees are truly a team, whether they act like it or not. Success comes when every member of an organization pulls his fair share of the workload.

A dangerous philosophical trend developed in the corporate world during the 1990s. People got so focused on the concept of leadership that they forgot about the other half of the success equation. Writers, corporate trainers, and novice consultants put all of the responsibility for positive change on the shoulders of an organization's leaders. While I believe that leaders must initiate change, it is then the responsibility of their followers to work cooperatively with leaders. Followers can act like a sail or an anchor as an organization attempts to navigate the new waters of change. If they choose to encourage their leaders and participate constructively in the change process, they can generate tremendous positive energy for the effort. Conversely, if followers choose not to cooperate, especially with a change initiative that is in their best interest, leaders naturally can become discouraged. No one, including those in leadership, wants to see his efforts sabotaged, ridiculed, or ignored by people around him. Unfortunately, this happens too often in business, ministry, and even family life. In many organizations, the relationship between leaders and followers is so strained that extensive team building must be done before positive change can occur. It is often necessary to go back into the past to discover what caused such rancorous relationships. This is like a trip through a bad section of town: it isn't pleasant, but you may have to go through it to get to your destination.

One of the most difficult tasks as a consultant is to help people in conflict move beyond problems of the past toward the promise of a united future.

The reason for this backtracking is fairly simple. In the early stages of change, people involved in the process often blame someone, especially someone from the other "side," for the current problems. This blame game is played by those in labor disputes and political groups, and between husbands and wives during marital conflicts. One of the most difficult tasks for me as a consultant is to help people in conflict move beyond problems of the past toward the promise of a united future. Experience has shown that when two groups are at odds, one party is no more guilty than the other. Many parents have needed the wisdom of Solomon when listening to one child's convincing story about a conflict with a sibling, only to have the other child give an equally convincing rebuttal minutes later. Final resolution comes only after the parents speak with both children at the same time. Only then is the real truth likely to be discovered. Only then can they begin reconciling the relationship.

But, imagine the problems that could occur if only one child was asked to bring reconciliation to the strained relationship. How successful would the reconciliation effort be if one child was expected to change his attitude about the other child, cooperate with that child, share possessions and encourage the other child, but the second child was allowed to persist in negative behavior? This would create a most unfair expectation on the first child and ultimately would cause him to resent the other child's lack of commitment to the reconciliation process.

I have found that this principle applies in conflicts between labor and management, one department and another, and certainly between leaders and followers at all levels of an organization. When one individual or group tries to change from adversary to ally without a corresponding commitment from the other side, the cooperative party often is taken advantage of.

I often tell a story about Teddy, a hunting dog that I owned years ago. He was an extremely responsive Golden Retriever that I purchased when he was just six weeks old. Within two years, he was trained to respond to hand signals in the field and would immediately obey my verbal instructions. This worked well until the day a large stray dog came into my yard and began to fight with Teddy. Hearing the commotion, I ran out and yelled, "No!" This was my dog's command to stop immediately whatever he was doing. Unfortunately, my dog obeyed and the stray dog did not. The stray proceeded to chew my defenseless dog up one side of his body and down the other. As I sent the stray dog on his way with a kick in the backside, I thought about the impact of my training on my canine friend. My dog did what was right, but his opponent did not. Why? The opponent was not trained to react the same way. Clearly, unless both animals stop on command, one of them stands to lose a lot of fur.

I have used this illustration to convince leaders and followers to stop "biting" each other and start working together for positive change. This is why it is so important to upgrade the attitudes and skills of *all* members of an organization as soon as possible in the change process. Once they are equipped with new methods of resolving conflict, communicating, listening, leading, and following, they begin to build the future together.

PROPER PERSPECTIVE

Obviously, our followers are neither children nor four-footed friends. These examples simply illustrate principles that otherwise may be difficult to grasp. Our followers are adult human beings who deserve respect and guidance from leaders. We should remember that they, too, have choices about where they will work, worship, and live. If leaders become oppressive or inherently unfair, followers often exercise their option to leave. Therefore, a leader must act in ways that encourage followers to align with his vision rather than waste time trying to force followers to submit to his will.

QUALITIES OF EFFECTIVE FOLLOWERS

Our organizational assessments have shown some fascinating facts about the qualities that leaders most appreciate in followers. Followers can model these qualities to make good impressions on leaders.

SELF-MOTIVATED

These followers actually take the lead during their workday. They understand the vision, mission, core values, and operating principles of their organization and apply this information when making decisions. These employees do not require extensive supervision to produce high-quality work. They show initiative and are willing to go above and beyond what is expected of them.

Contrast this employee with one who is unmotivated and unwilling to do more than what is required. This negative worker represented the majority of the employees in the automotive factory where I worked many years ago. One day, several of the overhead lights went out in the department next to mine. This did not present a serious problem because large skylights provided more than enough natural light for workers to continue safely. However, the supervisor followed the standard procedure for this situation and temporarily halted production. An electrician was called and the employees took a short break until he arrived to investigate. It soon became clear that the problem with the lights would take several hours to fix. It seemed logical that the employees simply would go back to work, right? But that didn't happen. With a mischievous grin, a less-motivated employee complained to the department supervisor that he could not work without lights. "Remember, safety first!" he smugly said, as if daring the supervisor to challenge his decision. The supervisor hesitated for a moment and, in so doing, lost all control.

There are people whose personal mission in life seems to be to convince the rest of us that we should be just as miserable as they are.

The employee proudly proceeded to a nearby break area, where he sat and sipped coffee from a vending machine. Soon, other employees made a similar pilgrimage to the break area. When the supervisor protested, the lazy employee said that his contract protected him from having to work in unsafe conditions and threatened to report this situation to the OSHA (Occupational Safety and Health Act) representative. The perplexed supervisor then asked the employees to help clean the department, since it needed extensive housekeeping. With one voice, the employees replied that they were machine operators, and department clean-up was not specifically written into their job descriptions.

What was the result of this standoff? The rest of us watched their entire department sit in the break area for the next six hours. They laughed, played cards, drank coffee, and generally enjoyed themselves. Some of these "workers" even slept while the rest of us remained on the job. At the end of the shift, they simply walked to the time clock and punched out. Their lack of motivation started a running battle between them and their embarrassed supervisor that was still raging years later.

POSITIVE ATTITUDE

Followers who remain positive about the organization and its future are rated very high by those in authority. These workers provide welcome relief from the whiners, complainers, and negative thinkers who haunt nearly every organization. Strange as it seems, there are people whose personal mission in life seems to be to convince the rest of us that we should be just as miserable as they are. While attitude may be hard to measure, everyone knows a bad one when they see it. Conversely, people who maintain a positive perspective on life and work are a joy to be around. These people lift the spirits and performances of those around them. Also, positive people do exceptionally well in a crisis, which makes them valuable allies for their leaders.

FLEXIBILITY

Leaders view followers who are overly rigid in their approach to work duties, schedules, and job requirements as uncooperative. For flexible followers, job descriptions serve as guidelines that may be expanded rather than a list of limitations. I realize that flexibility can be difficult, particularly in a union environment. However, today's rapidly changing world demands greater flexibility from followers—even unionized followers—if their organizations are to remain competitive. Ideally, employees will view well-conceived changes in their work routines as opportunities to gain stronger relationships with customers rather than personal inconveniences. Those who do not may become liabilities to their organizations and subsequently to their own careers.

I witnessed a sad example of this one day. My client's organization had built its success by responding quickly to customers' last-minute requests for products. Naturally, this meant that production schedules would change frequently—sometimes weekly or even daily. Whenever these changes occurred, most managers and employees accepted them without complaint. They correctly associated customer-initiated change with personal job security.

Despite his superior technical ability, the supervisor went the way of all dinosaurs that could not adapt.

One department's supervisor, however, had a very different reaction to these disruptions to his schedule. He would complain loudly about the inconvenience and about upper management's inability to manage properly. His flawed theory was that customers "pushing them around" caused the constant changes in production schedules. He would tell anyone who would listen that he had much better ideas about how to run the company. Like an infectious disease, his dissatisfaction soon was caught by others in his department; they began coughing out the same complaints about production schedule changes. Despite his superior technical ability, the supervisor went the way of all dinosaurs that could not adapt. He finally experienced vocational extinction. His manager replaced him with a person who had half his skills, but twice his tolerance for change.

TEAM PLAYERS

The most productive followers are those who can work effectively with peers. Since very few tasks are accomplished alone, each person must develop the ability to work cooperatively with others. If I could describe team players in one word, it would be *mature.* Team players control their egos, tend to be confident in their own abilities, and are willing to do their fair share of the work. The impact of team players on performance is phenomenal. A cohesive team often performs better than a group of people who have more skill but are unwilling to work together.

I was fortunate to be part of a semiprofessional football team that proved this point. Each week, our opponents had greater talent than we had. Some were faster, stronger, or more experienced, but we continued to defeat them for one simple reason: We played together. In the early games of the season, the newspapers described us as a "Cinderella" team. Evidently, this meant that our string of victories was more fairy tale than real life, and soon would end. They were wrong. We ultimately played the league's top team in the championship game and won the game handily. Team players can make a positive difference in any business, church, or family. Leaders with these types of followers spend the majority of their time pursuing their missions without having to serve as referees—or worse yet, baby-sitters—for the self-centered followers in their organizations.

TRUSTWORTHY

Leaders are comforted when they know they can trust their followers to be honest, productive, and dedicated to the organization's well-being. Conversely, followers who are dishonest, unproductive, and dedicated only to themselves can consume inordinate amounts of their leaders' time and energy. The vast majority of employees are truly dedicated and honest. However, a few followers spend their time creating innovative methods to take advantage of their companies. These people often are so crafty that they persist in their schemes for years—much to the displeasure of their leaders and peers.

I remember one such employee who was employed by my father during the 1960s at a large manufacturing firm. This man, whom I will call Geno, was a machine operator. Geno always had something better to do than to come to work. Over the years, he missed more time than any other employee who worked there. His excuses were legendary. Following an absence, Geno would often report that he had attended the funeral of one of his relatives. It was amazing how many second and third cousins he had, and how many of them died—regularly. Geno sometimes would get his lies crossed and report that some died more than once. As the years went by, his list of excuses grew in scope and complexity. He missed work several times because his house had been broken into, his dog had run away, his cat had been killed, and his car had broken down.

On the physical side, he reported headaches, fevers, colds, earaches, foot aches, and backaches. To support his scam, Geno also had a dishonest doctor who would sign notes confirming the ailments. This prevented company doctors from forcing him back to work, even though there was nothing physically wrong with him. At one point, Geno discovered a new ailment that even the company doctor was reluctant to check regularly: hemorrhoids. While he suffered only an extremely mild case, this soon became his favorite reason to miss work. With this newfound excuse, it seemed that Geno would continue to bilk his company for the duration of his stay there. However, like most cheats, Geno eventually got what was coming to him.

One day, his supervisor came up with a novel idea that would turn Geno's world upside down. Rather than arguing about the validity of Geno's claim of severe hemorrhoid problems, the supervisor actually began to sympathize with him. He asked Geno to bring in all of his doctor's reports about the severity of his delicate condition and assembled them into one file. The supervisor then listened to Geno's almost believable declaration that he would do *anything* to be able to return to work. Armed with the doctor's reports and Geno's stated desire to be well, the supervisor lovingly asked him to return the following day to continue the discussion. A smiling Geno showed up the next morning to find that his supervisor had taken the initiative to schedule Geno for hemorrhoid surgery at a nearby hospital. The surgery was to take place within the next two days, and it was a condition of continued employment for Geno. Finally, he was caught in his own web of lies and half-truths and had to submit to the surgery. Two weeks later, Geno returned to his job with a whole new perspective on work. He had truly learned . . . in the end.

In my own company, we have developed a team of men and women who know they can trust one another. My associates and office staff alike fill out their own time sheets and profit sharing information. They also schedule their own vacation time. This type of working relationship—founded upon a shared vision, mission, core values, and operating principles—needed a long time to develop. We also have spent sufficient time together to understand the motive of each person's heart, as well as individual strengths and weaknesses. This type of work environment is possible in any organization whose leaders invest time in developing strong, trust-based relationships.

THE ROLE OF TRAINING

A follower's performance is only as good as the education, training, and experiences that he brings to or receives in the organization. Some employees arrive on the doorstep of their employers fully prepared to produce high-quality work. However, many people have never been instructed in the proper way to align themselves with another's mission, follow someone else's lead, or even to work effectively with others. The organization then must provide the needed training, or limp along crippled by unproductive workers.

A follower's response to leadership can range from blind obedience to outright rebellion. In the first example, subordinates seem to function like mindless robots, blindly following any leader's directive—sometimes to their own destruction. The opposite involves people who refuse to submit to any mission other than their own. In other words, they work directly against their leaders.

In most situations, the proper form of followership is a balance somewhere between the two extremes. I encourage employees, church members, and citizens alike to learn about their leaders' visions, missions, core values, and methods of operation to see if what is important to their leaders is aligned with their own systems of values. Then, I suggest that followers give their leaders as much support as they comfortably can give. The followers should continue doing so unless they see the leaders beginning to stray from the agreed-on vision or core values. When this type of deviation occurs, I encourage followers to communicate directly with their leaders to help get them back on course . . . if they can do so without undue risk to themselves.

During times of drastic change or in organizations where the actions of leaders have created a low level of trust, I recommend that followers approach the future in at least a "hostile neutral" position. This odd term is one that I coined to let people know that they could withhold their full support without actively opposing a change effort that might ultimately benefit them. They can wait to see if the effort is beneficial for them and their organizations.

Regardless of past problems, it is important for followers to help eliminate barriers caused by poor interpersonal relationships with leaders. Leaders and followers alike should work to overcome the selfishness that is so prevalent in organizations today. In the modern workplace, there is often a reluctance to work together, share ideas, and team up on a variety of projects. This hide-your-answers mentality may be appropriate for an elementary education environment where daily grades are given for individual performances, but it is the worst possible approach for organizational excellence. In recent years, some colleges and universities have begun to assign team projects; however, it may be many years before leaders or followers arrive at our organizations ready to use this approach with coworkers.

A relatively small amount of team-building training is necessary to teach most people how to interact productively with peers. For this reason, I believe that every organization should expose all followers to a wide variety of training in interpersonal relations, problem solving, communication, and how to influence others. Once prepared with these new skills, most followers will provide support, encouragement, and expertise to their leaders as they pursue the organization's mission.

QUESTIONS AND REFLECTIONS

Business • Government • Ministry • Family • Personal

1. Do followers in your organization demonstrate self-motivation?

2. Do followers in your organization demonstrate positive attitudes?

3. Do followers in your organization demonstrate flexibility?

4. Do followers in your organization operate as team players?

5. What would be the impact on your organization if followers demonstrated these qualities to a greater degree?

THE MOLITOR DEVELOPMENTAL PROCESS

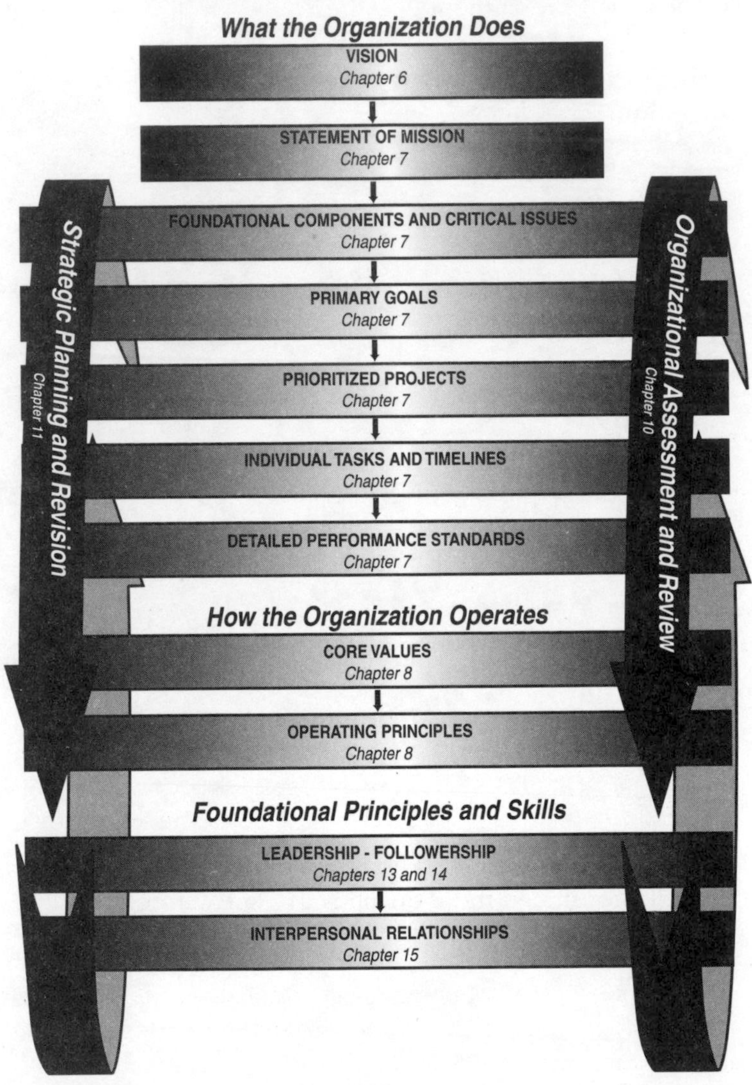

Chapter 15

BUILDING THE TEAM

Teams, teamwork, employee involvement, team building, and quality of work life—these concepts became part of mainstream corporate thinking during the 1970s and continue with us today. As with so many new concepts, businesses and other organizations joined the procession and tried to build teams. Unfortunately, many of them knew just enough about team building to be dangerous to themselves and their employees. Some destroyed their existing organizational structure to form a "team" environment. Some assembled groups of people to solve problems and called them "teams." Others did some basic team-building training without any real plan for how to make the training part of daily work life. All of these efforts gave an appearance of progress without making any real improvement in the organization.

Of course, with all of the interest—not to mention money—in this concept, a small army of team-building consultants and trainers sprang up like mushrooms to "help" the process. For awhile, it seemed that every unemployed manager with minimal experience felt qualified to consult with others about the fine points of team building. Public team-building seminars were offered by the hundreds, each event promising to teach attendees everything they needed to know about building teams. All of this for ninety-nine dollars or less—with coffee and donuts included. Some attendees learned the basics of team building, ate the donuts, and returned to work a bit wiser. Others returned to their organizations like moths looking for a flame. They immediately tried to force their peers to get with the team-building program, but to no avail. Within weeks, their initial zeal was squelched since those around them hadn't the foggiest idea of what all the fuss was about.

Sending a few representatives to a team-building seminar is as illogical as sending a husband to marriage counseling and expecting him to save a troubled marriage by himself. It just won't work. Team building takes place when *groups* of people begin to work more effectively together, not when a few enlightened people begin talking about it.

Many companies realized the folly of the piecemeal approach and simply plunged in to "do" team building without any outside assistance. The results were mixed. Typically, there was a lot of initial excitement that dissipated quickly when it became obvious that the approach wouldn't work. The reason for the early excitement is simple: Just the thought of teamwork is highly motivating for most people. Deep in our hearts, we earnestly desire to cooperate with others and to be part of something larger than ourselves. I believe this produces some initial success—or at least enthusiasm—for nearly all team-building efforts. However, without a clear understanding of the entire concept and a long-term, comprehensive plan for implementation, these initiatives are bound to fail quickly. Organizations that involve people in team initiatives without first building supportive relationships offer a cheap imitation of the genuine life-changing concept.

In reality, team building was, is, and always will be a very complex undertaking that must be planned carefully before tried. Team building is not an end, but, rather, it is undertaken as a means to better accomplish an organization's mission. It is extremely rare that team building alone is sufficient to make lasting improvements in any organization. As we have seen in previous chapters, an organization needs a number of elements in place for it to function properly. These include clear purpose and direction, effective leadership, core values, operating principles, a strategic plan, adequate systems, markets, and financing. No amount of training or even legitimate teamwork can compensate for glaring deficiencies in these areas. However, when team building is one component of an overall development effort, team building is the glue that holds the entire process together. Used in this manner, team building *will* produce incredible results in morale, productivity, and personal performance improvement.

BY THE WAY, WHAT IS A TEAM?

My working definition of a team is: Two or more people who are prepared, equipped, and committed to work together to achieve a common purpose. This definition suggests that a team may be a family, school system, department, corporation, or even a nation that seeks to maximize its positive influence in the world. Also, a team may be an entire organization, or a just part of the organization. For example, the members of a local church, including the leaders, can be considered a team. However, subgroups of the same church can be considered teams. There are teams of ushers, teachers, preschool workers, maintenance personnel, deacons, and elders who help achieve the overall mission as they complete their own group's goals.

Here is a simple truth: People working in effective teams accomplish more than an equal number of people working individually. True teamwork produces benefits in both productivity and personal satisfaction. Years ago, I heard one man's account of heaven and hell. He described hell as a banquet hall filled with millions of people. They were seated across from one another at tables covered with the most scrumptious food imaginable. Tantalizing sights and tempting aromas filled the hall.

There was one problem, however. The handles on the eating utensils were four feet long and could only be grasped at the very end. This made it virtually impossible for people to feed themselves. They could not get the food into their mouths. Their frustrations soon grew into anger and rage that lasted throughout all eternity. So much for hell.

At first glance, heaven seemed similar in every respect: It contained the same type of banquet hall, the same wonderful food, and the same long-handled utensils that could be grasped only at the very end. However, the people at the heavenly banquet tables were content. Instead of angry cries, laughter filled the hall. Close inspection showed the reason for their joy. Rather than trying to serve himself, each person used his utensils to serve someone across the table, who would then return the kindness.

While this story will never win a theological debate, it does make a solid point about teamwork. We get more accomplished when we work together and when we look for ways to serve those around us. Amen.

TEAMWORK OR WORK TEAMS?

Often, there is a great deal of confusion about the goal of a team-building effort. The concept of *teamwork* deals with new attitudes and enhanced interpersonal relationships. Conversely, the concept of *work teams* relates more to new structures and reporting relationships. Obviously, there is a huge difference between the two, but many organizations fail to see the difference. Companies throughout the world often arrange their people in a wide variety of new configurations, including a modified pyramid structure, multidisciplinary task force, self-directed work groups, product teams, and cross-functional work teams. People in these new structures may fight like cats and dogs, and still be accurately called a work team. All too often, these new structures yield few positive results. The real value comes when managers develop teamwork among the organization's members. Then they can achieve peak performance in a wide variety of organizational structures.

THE FOUNDATIONS OF TEAMWORK

Team-building training and development should focus on the primary elements of teamwork. The following are some of the basic foundations that need to be in place for any team's success.

CLEAR PURPOSE AND DIRECTION

Each team must understand its purpose and direction in order to maximize contribution to the mission. This will include an understanding of the organization's vision and mission, foundational components and critical issues, primary goals, priorities, and the role that each team member is to play in the organization's strategic plan. Chapters 6, 7, and 8 address these topics in detail.

EFFECTIVE LEADERSHIP

Team leaders generally determine the pace and performance of a team. Each team will have different leadership needs, so I use the term *effective leadership* to allow for a variety of approaches. Some teams need a great deal of instruction, guidance, and oversight. Others need a lot of freedom to accomplish their tasks. It is up to the team's leaders to determine what is needed to maximize its performance. Effective leadership is crucial because team members can never out-perform or compensate for incompetent leaders over an extended period of time. The foundations of leadership are covered in detail in chapter 13.

PRODUCTIVE INTERPERSONAL RELATIONS

The power to change an organization is unleashed when people work together. The greater the cooperation, the faster the organization can change. Conversely, in organizations where there is little cooperation, change is painfully slow. Real teamwork is easier to describe than to achieve, though, since people often tend to be independent, self-centered, and need time to develop trust in others. We rarely stop to consider viewpoints other than our own. Therefore, improving interpersonal relations skills of both leaders and followers is necessary to maximize the effectiveness of a change effort. In many ways, organizations are similar to blended families, one made up of a man and woman who got married after previous marriages. A friend of mine recently shared about the challenge he faced when he remarried. He and his new wife each had two children from previous marriages. All the children were young teenagers.

When they moved into their new house, there was a great deal of conflict among the children about what seemed to be even the smallest issues. Every question turned into a debate. Who sits in the "best" seats at the dinner table? Who gets the bedroom with the extra ten square feet of space? Who sits in the front seat of the car on the daily drive to school? These may appear to be irrelevant, but they are defining issues to displaced teenagers. At the root of each issue were the children's concerns about acceptance, status, security, and their sense of well-being. My friend reports that it took several months of training, coaching, and officiating by Dad and Mom before a relative calm descended upon their home.

This example is small in scale when compared to the conflict and turmoil found in most work environments. I have learned that it takes a lot of hard work to develop unity between just two individuals. Each additional person added to the mix increases both the problems and potential of the team exponentially. Like my friend's new family, organizations don't automatically unify just because its members share a common name, share similar values, and live or work under the same roof. True teamwork is a product of effective interpersonal relations among all team members.

The power to change an organization is unleashed when people work together on areas of agreement.

Interpersonal relations covers a variety of subjects, including teamwork, interdependence, cooperation, caring, communication, listening, and respect for others. These are qualities most of us appreciate in friends and family, but too often are absent in our organizational relationships. In part, this is because we send confusing messages to our children in their developmental years. In millions of homes around the world, parents teach their children to cooperate, share, and bond. Selfishness is frowned on; concern for others is encouraged. So far, so good.

Then, these children enter school and are taught to do their own work and not share information with others. Competition is encouraged. The children receive individual grades on report cards, individual honors for achievement, individual scholarships, and, ultimately, individual job offers. So why are we surprised that our organizations are filled with people who don't really know if they *should* work together, let alone *how* to work together? This is one reason why having clear core values and operating principles is so vital for every organization. They clarify expectations about the company's approach to teamwork, thereby releasing, encouraging, and, in some cases, warning employees of the need to work together.

Fortunately, most people respond positively to some basic teaching on teamwork and immediately apply it to their work and personal lives. In countless training sessions, I have found that people must be convinced that it is to their advantage to cooperate with peers. We should make no mistake that, for many people, cooperation with others is not natural. It is a foreign act that must be taught and reinforced continually after the training has been completed.

We receive individual grades on our report cards, individual honors for achievement, individual scholarships, and, ultimately, individual job offers. So why are we surprised that our organizations are filled with people who don't really know if they should work together, let alone how to work together.

Several years ago I designed a business simulation that proves the futility of internal competition and the value of internal cooperation. Often, we use this simulation as the initial training exercise in our seminars. The exercise is simple but effective. First, we create a mythical corporation, complete with products, schedules, and financial concerns. I divide participants into different corporate divisions. Then, each separate division interacts with others in a simulated business scenario to make a profit or loss. The profit or loss results from a pattern of decisions that the divisions make over a period of time.

The exercise is designed so that individual divisions lose money whenever they compete against each other and make significant profit whenever they cooperate. Invariably, the divisions work against each other in the early stages of the exercise, resulting in anger, frustration, and mistrust. Eventually, one department risks cooperating with the others, and they all begin to prosper. Following the exercise, we talk about the impact of internal competition on the participants' actual organization. Once they see how normal—foolish—it is to work against each other, they commit to overcome this tendency and cooperate for the benefit of all.

COMMUNICATION/LISTENING SKILLS

It is vital that each member of an organization be highly skilled in verbal communication and listening skills. Several years ago, a $150-million satellite became galactic garbage when it did not properly eject from its booster rocket after launch. According to the manufacturer, it failed to separate properly because *missed communication between two workers* caused the wrong chamber to be wired for separation. Ironically, this flying failure was a communication satellite. This spectacular example typifies the communication breakdown that happens each day in virtually every organization on this planet. Since words and concepts are subject to interpretation, we will never eliminate miscommunication entirely. However, with proper training and monitoring of the communication process, we can improve dramatically our chances for success.

One very important aspect of the communication process is effective listening. Without it, organizations suffer from an overabundance of information being sent, but little actually received and used to advance the mission. It is often necessary to remind even the most senior members of an organization of the importance of these basic topics. At first glance, foundational teachings may be considered too elementary for high-level leaders, but our organizational assessments have proven many times that top officials speak above their followers' level of comprehension rather than with them or, worse yet, speak down *to* them. This creates countless interpersonal and performance problems that easily could be avoided with proper communication. In similar fashion, employees must learn to effectively communicate with and listen to their peers, leaders, customers, and suppliers.

PROBLEM-SOLVING AND DECISION-MAKING SKILLS

As individuals, we develop problem-solving and decision-making skills through our training, education, and life experiences. We use these skills each day to avoid life's pitfalls and achieve personal goals. However, it is a challenge to combine the insights of two or more individuals to solve problems that impact their organization. Personal agendas, unchecked egos, poor data collection methods, and lack of a systematic approach to problem solving are just a few causes of the poor performance. In successful teams, people have learned to use interpersonal skills and group problem-solving techniques to attack organizational problems rather than one another. The concept of consensus decision making also needs to be clearly understood for organizations to prosper. Throughout the world, an incredible amount of time is wasted in meetings in which participants are unable to make decisions together. Once problem solving teams are trained, they quickly can resolve complex issues that drain the vitality from their organizations. Problem solving and decision making will be covered in more detail in the following chapter.

TRUST

People today are less trusting than in the past, and for good reason. We have often placed our trust in people who later disappointed, deceived, or demeaned us. In recent years, we have seen the downfall of leaders in the political, business, and religious arenas. Millions of people who have entered into marriage found that their "partner for life" was not serious about the wedding vows. These betrayals produce histories that we drag into new situations and relationships. Therefore, we must teach people how to be trustworthy and how to trust others in the workplace. Team members can develop trust as they discuss goals, concerns, and personal values with one another. Granted, it takes time and honest communication to close the book on some of our histories, but it *can* be done. In a team-oriented work environment, trust is born when we establish an agreed-to set of core values and operating principles. Then, trust matures as team members demonstrate their concern for the well-being of others on a daily basis.

Conflict Resolution Methods

In any relationship, conflict is normal. If handled correctly, conflict can be extremely positive. However, we often choose destructive methods of addressing conflicts that arise in our organizations. While there may be many variations, there are really only five options to choose from to address conflict. The first four leave much to be desired. We may (1) ignore conflict, (2) concede to the other person's position without any discussion, (3) become confrontational, or (4) develop a middle-of-the-road compromise that actually satisfies no one.

Rational people have discovered that the only approach to conflict resolution that makes sense is cooperation. This method encourages everyone involved in the conflict to share their perspectives, facts, issues, and opinions without trying to drag others to their side or position. Handled in this manner, truth resolves the conflict, not emotion, politics, or intimidation. Often, training is required to teach a cooperative approach to conflict resolution. A trained team of people can see the vast majority of their conflicts resolved to everyone's satisfaction.

Proper Skills, Knowledge and Abilities

A team's good intentions and positive team spirit can never overcome a lack of skill or knowledge from its members. When my sons, Christopher and Steven, were in junior high school, I had the pleasure of coaching their basketball team. During one tournament, we were scheduled to play against a team that looked like they would be difficult to beat. Our opponents entered the gymnasium wearing designer warm-up suits in matching colors. Their game uniforms were obviously very expensive compared to our team's plain blue shirts. This team's pregame activities were strictly controlled by coaches who barked orders to the young men as if they were competing in the world championship series. Things looked bleak for our team.

When the game started, things began to look different. Despite all of the outward appearances to the contrary, however, our opponents did not have the basic skills necessary to compete with our team. They made many fundamental mistakes. When it came to pure athletic abilities, my team was far better. The result was that we won the game handily.

The application to organizations is simple. All members of the team must have the skills and abilities necessary to complete their tasks well. This should be a primary concern for all team leaders who want to win their own type of corporate championship.

Sufficient Resources, Information, Supplies, and Equipment

Let's stay with the basketball analogy. Imagine the results if I had sent our team onto the court without basketball shoes. What if some players were barefooted, and others wore heavy work boots? Rather than cotton shirts and shorts, what if our players wore long pants and overcoats? Let's make it ridiculous: imagine them wearing woolen mittens while trying to dribble, pass, and shoot the ball. When the game begins, what if I fail to tell them which plays to run, or what positions my team members should play? What is likely to happen if our opponents are as skilled as we are, but are properly dressed for the game and their coaches provide them with the information needed to compete? Under these conditions, who would win the game? Obviously, our opponents would. Why? The reasons are obvious: We were poorly equipped and lacked information we needed to compete. All too often, teams in business, government, and other organizations lose for similar reasons. Every team member needs the basic equipment, information, and other resources to get the job done properly.

FAIR PERFORMANCE EVALUATION, RECOGNITION, AND REWARD SYSTEMS

Here is a foundational truth: Teams are formed to *do* something. For example, teams in manufacturing operations produce products. Teams of firemen put out fires and save lives. Teams in restaurants provide both a product and a service by serving food to their customers. Teams that fail to produce tangible results should be disbanded . . . or recommissioned as political committees so that their lack of productivity won't be noticed as much!

Each team's efforts ultimately result in a product, a service, or both. These products or services provide the basis for the team's performance evaluation and rewards. Team members need leaders who provide clear expectations, feedback, recognition, encouragement, and tangible rewards for their efforts. The best teams receive feedback on their performance regularly. These actions keep the team motivated and operating at peak performance.

UNITED WE STAND

The team-building concepts listed in this chapter can revolutionize an organization as leaders and followers together apply the knowledge to improve relations with customers, suppliers, and one another. Any organization that has come this far in the developmental process has leaders who have begun to realize some significant improvements in individual and corporate performance. The mission has been set and the operating principles are becoming a way of life. Leaders are providing guidance and followers are responding. Strong interpersonal relationships are forming. Now almost everyone is responding to organizational challenges as competent, mature adults. The power of agreement is evident. Yet there is one more component that needs to be developed to ensure ongoing excellence: Problem solving.

QUESTIONS AND REFLECTIONS

Business • Government • Ministry • Family • Personal

1. How do members of your organization demonstrate teamwork?

2. How do members of your organization demonstrate a *lack* of teamwork?

3. What causes people in your organization to work together?

4. What causes people in your organization *not* to work together?

5. What would be the impact of increased cooperation and teamwork in your organization?

THE MOLITOR DEVELOPMENTAL PROCESS

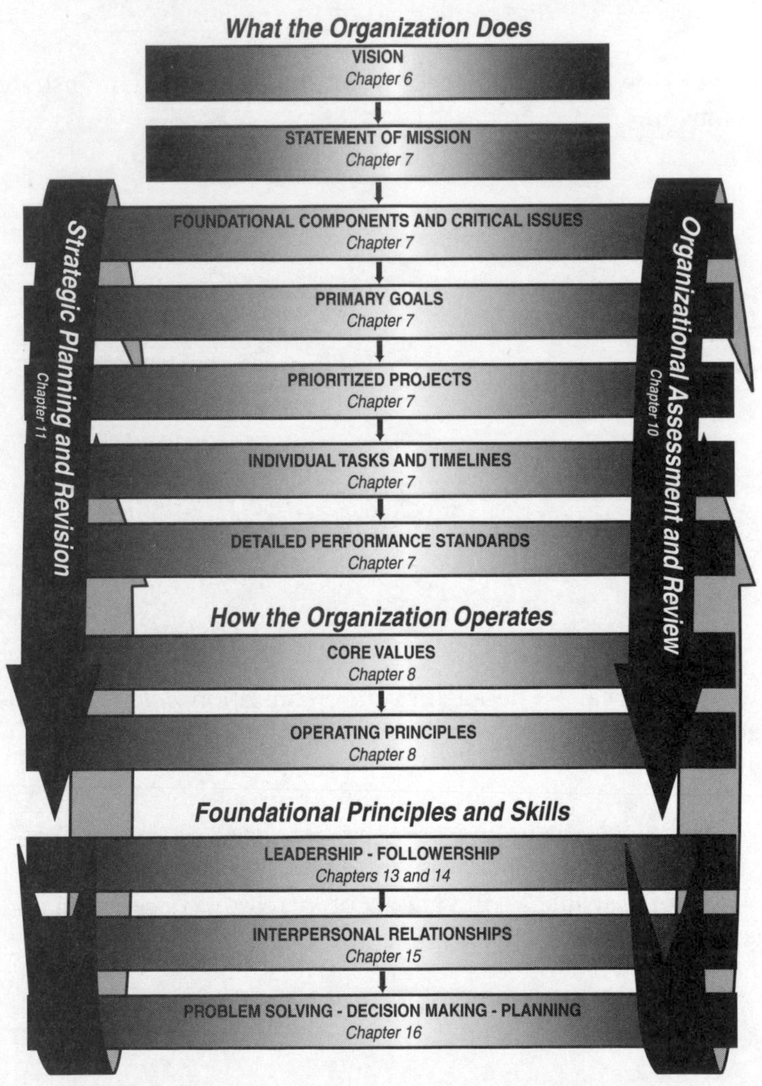

CHAPTER 16

PROBLEM SOLVING AND DECISION MAKING

Shouldn't problem solving be easier than what it is, especially since we face so many problems each and every day of our lives? Sometimes we solve one problem, only to create an even bigger one.

I recall hearing about a wealthy gentleman living in the northern United States who did just that. He had grown tired of shoveling snow off his sidewalk each winter; he planned to solve this problem permanently when he built a new house. His innovative solution was simple: When he constructed his majestic new home, he installed heating pipes under his driveway and sidewalks. According to his design, the pipes would heat the concrete during the winter to melt any snow that dared to fall on his domain. When the first heavy snowfall came, he excitedly turned on his heating system and waited for the results. His system worked to perfection; his was the only sidewalk in the neighborhood to remain free of snow. The man went to sleep confident that his neighbors soon would flock to his property to marvel at his new invention.

The next morning he awoke to find that he was half right in his prediction. It seems that his neighbors' *dogs* found his snow-free sidewalks an ideal place to relieve themselves. This was a welcome change from all of those cold, high snowdrifts to which the dogs were accustomed. The man's four-legged neighbors liked this innovation so much that they came to show their appreciation daily. That winter, the gentleman had more to shovel than just snow.

PROBLEM SOLVING AND CHANGE

Every organization experiencing positive change encounters many problems along the way. This is normal, natural, and can even be extremely positive if the problems are resolved properly. The secret is to have all members of the organization ready, willing, and able to participate in problem solving and decision making on a daily basis. Progress is severely handicapped when leaders try to solve all problems themselves, make all decisions, and have all the answers for virtually everything that impacts the organization.

Superman was a comic-book hero, not an organizational leader of today. Leaders who play the role of resident expert in all things soon render themselves ineffective. Why? Conditions change so rapidly that one leader cannot keep up with them all. Problems must be solved *as* they arise to keep the organization moving ahead. Most problems can be solved by trained followers who know their authority, boundaries, and what resources are available to them. An organization's change process can accelerate to light speed once its members have mastered problem solving, decision making, and planning—and are authorized to use these skills as they see fit.

THE PROBLEM WITH PROBLEM SOLVING

Meetings. Every organization in the world has meetings. Some meetings are conducted to communicate new information. Others are for discussing opportunities that may benefit the organization. Some meetings take place in crowded hallways and last for a few moments, while others may be held in exotic locations and last for several weeks. Regardless of where they are held or how long they last, many meetings are designed to do one thing: solve problems. Meetings that fail to accomplish this are often a monumental waste of time, money, and human resources.

A good measure of the success of any meeting is the reaction of people who attend them. Meeting announcements often are met with groans, complaints, or silent sulking. Why? Too many meetings fail to achieve their goals. Too many problem-solving sessions actually create more problems than they solve. Many degenerate into circular discussions that produce too few tangible results. Isn't it interesting that these discussions often last as long as the meeting was scheduled for? Participants rush back to their real work wondering why they were asked to waste valuable time on such folly. Fortunately, it doesn't have to be this way. There are some very tangible reasons for this lack of productivity.

The efforts of many groups are hindered by intragroup intimidation, hidden agendas, lack of clear direction, poor interpersonal relationships, and/or a lack of basic problem-solving skills. While each person comes to the organization with some degree of analytical skill, he uses a slightly different approach to problem solving than others use. These different approaches often conflict, explaining why so many simple problems are difficult to solve in a group setting.

WHY FORM TEAMS TO SOLVE PROBLEMS?

This may come as a shock to some people, but a committee or team of people should not analyze every problem. In fact, most problems should be addressed by the people responsible for the area affected by the problem. It is common for companies involved in problem-solving training to initially refer every problem to a team for resolution. Obviously, this can waste time and other resources. It also may produce a lower-quality decision than if the person closest to the problem simply had made the decision.

This may come as a shock to some people, but a committee or team of people should not analyze every problem.

It takes time to learn which problems to assign to a team and which to assign to an individual. While it can be difficult to arrive at solutions in a group setting, some problems are ideally suited for a team solution. For instance, when problems impact more than one person, department, or area of operation, a team may be very effective. Also, when companies attempt to improve overall product quality, they must analyze their entire work process from the arrival of raw materials to delivery of finished goods to customers. This requires that representatives from many different areas come together to analyze and make decisions that will affect each of them. Under these circumstances, there is a lot of truth to the old saying: Two heads are better than one. The modern version of this saying deals with the term *synergy,* which says that one plus one is *greater* than two. In other words, when two or more people combine their insights about a complex situation, the results should be better than if they had tried to analyze it separately. This synergy happens every day in our businesses, churches, governments, and families.

Not long ago a client of ours was having a costly problem with contaminants in their products. These chemical products were packaged in fifty-gallon drums and sent by rail or truck across the country. Some of the company's most knowledgeable experts studied the situation and concluded that there were only two possible stages in manufacturing and delivery where contamination could occur. The experts began to focus their entire problem-solving efforts on these two stages.

First, they lectured employees who handled the material on the importance of being careful. This produced no change in product quality. Next, they purchased new equipment to load and seal the drums, but customers still complained about contaminants in the product. This frustrating pattern of trial and error continued for months. During this same period of time, a group of production employees was being trained in our problem-solving method, and decided to study this problem as part of the training course. When they completed a detailed process chart on the problem, everyone was amazed to learn that there were at least *eighteen* different stages in manufacturing and delivery where contaminants could get into their products. Their findings were shared with the personnel who had been studying the problem. Within weeks the problem was resolved permanently.

SUCCESSFUL PROBLEM SOLVING

A meeting or problem-solving session should be one of the most exciting parts of any workday. The potential is astronomical when two or more people share their knowledge, wisdom, and insights. This is where the true power of agreement can be released. Many times I have observed trained groups of leaders and followers solve serious problems that plagued their organizations for years. These groups have been successful over long periods of time and continue to discover millions of dollars in cost savings, streamline work processes, and to create new approaches to customer service.

Problem-solving efforts can succeed only when the people involved are properly prepared. It is crucial that all members of an organization use a common approach and agreed-on terms when attempting to solve problems. The basic logic and sequence of problem solving can be learned quickly and used for a lifetime. It is truly amazing what people accomplish with these problem-solving tools and a commitment to work together.

Any organization that has followed the developmental process outlined in this book has arrived at an exciting juncture where problem-solving efforts can produce some incredible results. Goals and priorities are clear, which makes it easy to identify problems that could hinder the mission. Interpersonal conflicts are at a minimum so people are able to sit and reason together without personal attacks. They are ready to be trained in a powerful process called *problem solving*.

THE PROBLEM-SOLVING PROCESS

In the mid-1980s, I noticed that much of the material on problem-solving training being produced was difficult for people to understand in a short period of time. Also, some terms added more confusion than clarity for the learners. In response, I designed the following seven-step problem-solving process that is easy to learn and use.

Step 1—Identify the Problems. The first step in problem solving is to identify clearly each problem by stating its impact, when it began, and if the cause of the problem is known or unknown.

Step 2—Rank the Problems. Once a list of problems has been compiled, the problems must be listed in priority order. This can be a challenge when more than one person is involved because of differences in perception of each problem's importance. A simple method of ranking the problems is used to avoid endless discussions fueled by personal agendas.

Step 3—Identify Probable Causes. At this step, people collect the information necessary to discover what has caused the problem. Different methods are taught for general, process, and people problems.

Step 4—Confirm Actual Cause. In this step, various charts, graphs, statistical process control charts, flow diagrams, and other tools are used to confirm the actual cause or causes of the problem. Each person involved in problem solving needs to learn how to create each type of data-collection tool and how to interpret them.

Step 5—Set Solution Goals. All too often, solutions are implemented that solve the original problem but create a larger problem somewhere else in the organization. This can be avoided by setting specific goals for each solution. These goals are used to determine if a proposed solution is ideal, acceptable, or unacceptable.

Step 6—Decide on a Solution. Most problems will have more than one solution. Therefore, each alternative needs to be analyzed to determine cost, return on investment, time to implement, and impact on other parts of the organization. Then the most appropriate solution is selected for implementation.

Step 7—Develop an Action Plan. Many proposed solutions fail because of poor planning prior to implementation. This final step of the problem-solving process teaches the importance of clear assignment of responsibilities, timelines, documentation, and follow-up to ensure that the solution has actually solved the problem.

THE PURPOSE OF TRAINING

Problem-solving training should always help people develop a logical, systematic approach to problem analysis. Once this approach has been mastered, it can be applied to virtually any problem situation in a person's work or personal life. In many instances, the understanding of a systematic problem-solving process is just as valuable as having detailed knowledge about a particular product or work process. Problem-solving training provides an excellent foundation for some advanced learning of statistical methods of quality control. Without a basic understanding of the problem-solving process, a great deal of time and resources can be wasted in the pursuit of quality.

Some employees forgot that management wanted quality parts, not quality charts.

In the mid-1980s, many companies got their employees involved in statistical process control (SPC). I recall one organization that sent all of its managers, supervisors, and production employees to two days of training on this topic. The training was introductory at best, and it certainly did not prepare the work force to be proficient in SPC. Corporate management saw it differently, though. As soon as everyone had been trained, they required employees to begin to draw SPC charts for each machine in their operation. Naturally, many of the employees could not remember how to plot the points correctly on the charts, or even why they were doing it in the first place. During one visit to this company, I was amazed to see that some employees literally had drawn points and lines off the charts and onto the wall that held the chart, without making any adjustments on their machines to correct the obvious quality problem! They forgot that management wanted quality *parts,* not quality *charts.* After some additional targeted training in theory, statistics, and a complete understanding of the basic problem-solving process, they became effective in their quest for quality.

I recall another client that made complex medical implant devices. The medical device industry is highly competitive, with new products being designed and introduced into the marketplace regularly. The first company to commercialize a new product receives the patent and subsequent profits while its competitors fall behind. This particular company's engineering department had the finest high-tech computers, computer-aided design/computer-aided manufacturing "CAD/CAM" software, and the latest training in how to use them.

One day, they ran into a problem with a hip-joint replacement device that put their production at a virtual standstill. For more than a week, senior engineers labored over the problem without positive results. They did the majority of their work on a central computer station that was located near Steven, a recently hired engineer. This young man had just graduated from college and was considered by senior engineers as too new to be of much help. As days went by, Steven could hear the heated discussions that raged as the experts worked to solve the problem. Whenever they would break for lunch, Steven very carefully would look over the data that they had been analyzing. He began to examine systematically the production process from its initial stages to completion, even though he had never been involved with the product. Soon, Steven's systematic thinking uncovered a tiny flaw in the process that the senior engineers had missed. When he finally made his suggestion to the group, they were amazed. His step-by-step approach made it possible to solve the problem and commercialize the product ahead of his company's competitors.

Let me share a word about experts. I am a firm believer in the importance of highly trained, specialized individuals. These people are like deep pools from which others can drink. However, I also am a firm believer that *every* person is an expert in his particular field, position, area, or job. Individual superstars rarely win championships—it takes every member of a team to bring about success. Often, innovation and invention come from ordinary people with extraordinary insight. Since we are all experts in at least one area of life, so we would do well to learn from one another.

I have found that successes like Steven's discovery can become a way of life for any organization whose leaders take the time to train its members in problem solving and then provide them with opportunities to use their newly acquired skills. No longer will problems linger until the top 5 percent of the organization can address them. In this new environment, as soon as a problem surfaces, it is addressed and resolved by the people closest to the situation. The organizations that use their people this way soon experience a wonderful transition. Once existing problems are solved, the focus changes to problem prevention and innovation. Like an army of excited inventors, people now use their formidable skills to anticipate problems, improve on existing solutions, and develop new products and services. At this point, the competition had better join that organization because it will never beat it!

QUESTIONS AND REFLECTIONS

Business • Government • Ministry • Family • Personal

1. What is your organization's approach to problem solving? Is it effective?

2. To what extent has problem solving and decision making been allowed at the lower levels of your organization?

3. Have all members of your organization been trained in problem solving and decision making? What is the impact?

4. Do some problems reoccur in your organization? Why?

5. Are meetings in your organization effective? How could they be made more effective?

CHAPTER 17

A NEW WAY OF LIFE

One New Year's Eve, I noticed an intriguing trend in the advertisements on television. Strangely absent was the endless stream of ads for some necessities of life, such as biscuits, breath mints, and toilet bowl cleansers. In their place was an absolute blitz of advertisements designed to capture the attention of the thousands of people making resolutions for change in the coming year. Ads promoted products for weight loss, exercise equipment, vitamins, discount fitness centers, and no less than three different products to help people stop smoking. Product sponsors knew that these ads on New Year's Eve would generate millions of dollars from an army of people who sincerely wanted to change their lifestyles. I am certain that some individuals seized the moment to become fat-free, smoke-free, and cholesterol-free for the rest of their lives. More power to them.

Sadly, I am just as certain that the majority fell back into their old habits in record time.

It seems that the advertisers held a similar conviction. By the first of February, the commercials featured candy bars and reclining lounge chairs once again. Why did they change? Because the advertisers knew that by February, most resolutions were only vague memories and people were ready to return to their unhealthy routines. How common it is for us to set goals for change when we are inspired or under pressure, only to forget about them when the pressure is off.

Consider Darnell, a heart attack victim, lying in a hospital emergency room trying to cope with the assault on his senses. Doctors and nurses race around the room as they work to save his life. He remembers the screaming sirens and flashing ambulance lights that woke up his sleepy neighborhood just minutes earlier. His wife, Shirley, flashes through his mind, then his children, little Chris and Jenifer. The oxygen mask muffles his words, but he silently prays: "Oh God, get me through this and I promise to change!" Exhausted, he slips into a dream.

The next day he awakens to learn that God has answered his prayer. He has another chance at life. Now come the promises, vows, and resolutions. Highly motivated, Darnell commits to change his diet and exercise every day to avoid another attack. For the first few months after leaving the hospital, he abstains from the fatty foods that helped clog his arteries. He faithfully jogs two miles each day. Soon he begins to feel better. After several months, he is breathing easier and has dropped twenty-five pounds. People say that he even *looks* better.

Strange as it seems, this may be the worst thing that could happen to him so early in his recovery. Feeling and looking better are symptoms of change but not the change itself. This is a most crucial time for Darnell. His future literally hangs in the balance. Why? Because at this point he is tempted to slow or to stop his personal process of change. The regression begins in small ways. Perhaps the two-mile run becomes a one-mile stroll as the couch and television become appealing again. The strict diet gives way to occasional cheating with junk food and so on. Soon he is in danger of having a second—and possibly fatal—heart attack. Darnell's only hope is to transform his change program into a new lifestyle.

In the same way, organizations are in danger after experiencing some success with change. There will be a temptation to back off on some of the commitments that have been made. In business, perhaps one of the leaders begins to mistreat followers, or perhaps employees let their quality standards down. Government leaders may be enticed to squander time, money, and other resources on projects other than those that support their stated missions. In the home, parents who have made commitments to spend more quality time with their children are tempted to work just a few more hours each week.

Organizations are in danger after experiencing some success with change.

Is it possible to guarantee that people trying to change will never slip back into their old ways? Obviously not, but I want to offer some encouragement to those who begin the process of change. I have learned that the chances of long-term success increase exponentially when the original need for change is remembered and when the progress is monitored on a regular basis. Several issues must be monitored and adjusted for change to become a new way of life.

Purpose and Direction. An organization's or individual's purpose and direction must be monitored regularly. Like explorers traveling through new territory, we need to make sure we are headed in the proper direction. We must make sure our vision, mission, goals, and priorities remain properly aligned. They should be checked regularly, at least once every six months for larger organizations, and much more often for smaller companies, churches, and family groups. I recommend that leaders schedule this checkup on their staff meeting agendas so that the checkup does not get lost among the inevitable daily distractions.

While the mission provides the organization with direction, core values provide it with protection.

Core Values. Honesty, integrity, quality of work, and concern for others are examples of core values. These values must be evaluated regularly or they will degenerate into meaningless buzzwords and phrases without substance. While the vision and mission provide the organization with direction, the core values provide it with protection. Core values are the first line of defense against temptation to compromise or abandon the very foundations of the organization's culture. Remember, the assault on our core values is continual. Dishonest salespeople try to bribe their way into the organization's supply budget. Lobbyists push politicians to vote for legislation that favors the lobbyist's cause. Manufacturers are tempted to sell products that are not quite up to acceptable standards. A pastor is asked to tone down his sermons by the wealthiest member of his small congregation. A family member is hired instead of a more qualified outsider. The list of potential pitfalls is endless. Yet there is never a valid reason for compromising on core values—only excuses.

There is never a valid reason for compromising on core values—only excuses.

The safest way to guard against cultural erosion is to monitor the core values of the organization constantly. This is accomplished by regular self-assessment and from discussions about the values with customers, suppliers, employees, volunteers, and anyone else who can give unbiased observations. Self-assessment can be a bit tricky though. We often act like the overweight man who pulls in his stomach while standing in front of a mirror. He walks away convinced of his fitness, but others have a different view. We need to make sure that our self-analyses are done on performance rather than good intentions. Our real core values are those that we actually demonstrate, not the ones we intend to demonstrate. I am a firm believer in the importance of conducting exit interviews with those who are leaving an organization. Those are the people who have little to lose by telling the truth about the organization, and they may expose potential blind spots.

Our real core values are those that we actually demonstrate, not the ones we intend to demonstrate.

In recent years, we have learned that when a person performs a behavior for approximately twenty-eight days in a row, it becomes a habit. This should encourage anyone who has struggled with a new diet or has tried to quit smoking. It is also good news for people involved in organizational change. The principle is the same, although it will take considerably longer than twenty-eight days to transform a nation, business, church, or family. The truth is, when something is done consistently over a period of time, it becomes ingrained. What begins as a novelty becomes a habit, and ultimately transcends into a new way of life. As core values become part of an organization's daily operation, these values build its inner culture. They are the heart, soul, and conscience of the organization. Leaders must guard the organization's foundational values as if its very existence depended on them—because in fact, it does.

Operating Principles. As we have learned, operating principles are actually core values in action. They are the visible manifestation of an organization's basic beliefs. They define how members of an organization are to interact with one another, and also clarify how products and services are provided to customers. When acted on over an extended period of time, these principles literally make up the outer or visible culture of a nation, business, or family. Therefore, they must be established and adhered to by the majority of people involved, or the culture will change for the worse.

Broad concepts such as quality, productivity, commitment to excellence, respect for others, and continuous improvement must be translated into specific actions that can be carried out by virtually every member of an organization. These actions then should be included with other bottom-line measurements to evaluate individual performance and to determine which members of the organization qualify for promotion and other rewards.

Leaders must guard the organization's foundational values as if its very existence depended on them—because it does.

Performance Evaluation Methods. Each member of an organization is responsible to perform certain duties related to the organization's mission. Therefore, it is important that leaders fairly and accurately evaluate the performance of each person. Also, it is vital that the evaluation of performance be done using some very objective and measurable standards. This approach helps foster cooperation among the followers and avoids perceptions of favoritism. Unfortunately, a common alternative today is to subjectively force rank employees into groups of winners and losers on an annual basis. When using this approach, organizations classify their employees into four or five categories, such as excellent, good, fair, poor, and failing. This type of ranking is generally done without clearly defined standards of performance. The so-called logic behind this approach to performance improvement is mystifying. It misses the mark in two ways.

First, it violates one of the foundational principles of positive reinforcement that relates to timing. Specifically, an annual performance evaluation delays the appropriate instruction, corrective comments, and/or encouragement from the leadership for up to twelve full months. It is a form of organizational insanity for any leader to allow an employee or volunteer to perform at poor or failing levels for a week, let alone an entire year, without trying to improve his work. Second, this method divides the organization by comparing the performance of one person to that of another, rather than comparing performance to a set of established standards, goals, or objectives. Using this flawed approach, one of the starting five players of a world championship basketball team would be considered a failure and a detriment to the team. Obviously, no professional coach would do such a thing, but this often is done in the corporate world.

Imagine the impact of the annual forced ranking approach if used by parents to evaluate family "performance." My wife and I have four children. If using this method, we would be forced to label one child as excellent and the others as good, fair, and failing. This would be unfair to 75 percent of our children—as well as inaccurate, since each child has demonstrated more than acceptable levels of industry, civility, love, and commitment to our family, their schoolwork, and household duties during the past year. Also, it is absurd to think that we would observe a child's misdeeds over an extended period of time without corrective comment. Imagine sitting with each child once a year to read a list of the past year's failures. If we happened to remember that the child had done something positive during that same period it might be mentioned, but the opportunity for immediate reinforcement would have been lost. So, obviously, under this approach our children would learn nothing from their "leaders," and their poor performances would be a liability to our family's well-being.

Perhaps we can learn a lesson about performance evaluation from my children's elementary school teachers. Their approach is simple, yet infinitely more effective than that of many corporate leaders. In school, each assignment is evaluated and graded daily. This way, if a child has a problem with a new concept, the instructor provides immediate help so the student does not fall behind. Also, each assignment is graded on established standards, so there is no need to force rank the students. The individual assignment grades provide the basis for a report card that is issued every nine weeks. At this same time, instructors arrange meetings with children and their parents to confirm and clarify any concerns about the child's performance. At the end of the school year, awards are given for outstanding performances in academics. Unlike the corporate world, this "annual performance review" has no surprises because each student's performance has been evaluated and discussed regularly. This simple approach can be modified easily to work in any organization.

My research confirms that the annual performance review and forced ranking were developed in response to a lack of leadership interaction with followers. Also, leaders were reluctant to give followers any bad news about their performances or they showed favoritism to a select few employees. Evidently, it was easier for many managers to declare everyone's performance acceptable and move on rather than tell the truth. Frustrated top management finally instituted an annual forced ranking to coerce managers and supervisors to talk with their followers about improved performance. They identified the right problem, but sadly came up with the wrong solution.

While no method of performance evaluation is flawless, the process can be made more accurate and productive. It requires two essential components: clear performance standards and leadership awareness of each follower's strengths and weaknesses. It is crucial that leaders establish performance standards that are clearly understood by everyone involved. These standards are used to measure all aspects of employee performance. When leaders have firsthand knowledge of followers' performances, they can reward, promote, discipline, and encourage them appropriately. There is no need to force rank employees, volunteers, or other followers using this method.

On a daily basis, each employee's performance falls into one of three categories: ideal, acceptable, or unacceptable. When monitored over time, these daily ratings soon make up a positive or negative trend. If the performance is negative or unacceptable, then the employee is offered help to improve. This may include coaching, counseling, job assistance, training, or transfer to a more suitable position. If a positive trend is sustained, then the employee's performance is classified as either ideal or acceptable. The positive performance is reinforced as leaders encourage the productive follower on a daily or weekly basis. The ideal performers are the first to be considered for promotion, positive transfer, additional duties, and/or monetary increases. The acceptable performers are the next group to receive promotion consideration and possible monetary rewards.

Recognition and Rewards. When organizations change, so should their basic approach to recognition and rewards. The people who most deserve to be promoted or rewarded financially are those who work productively toward the mission, demonstrate the core values, and live by the agreed upon operating principles. Those who fail to do so need to be trained, educated, coached, counseled, disciplined, or when all else fails, dismissed—but not rewarded. I have seen companies make great strides towards excellence, only to fall back for one simple reason: They promoted people who were not supporters of the change. Others in the organization perceived this as a signal from top management that the change process was just a passing fad and would never become a way of life.

Order and Discipline. Most things in this world naturally slow down, pull apart, break down, or degenerate. Mighty mountains erode over a period of time. Roaring rivers that spill down hillsides eventually slow their pace and settle as they reach the sea. The physical strength and vitality of a man's youth soon surrender to the inevitable aging process. In like fashion, some people's performance, behavior, or attitude will begin to fade without proper maintenance. While many people have the inner strength to overcome this tendency, others do not. This is true in all types of organizations. Employees let their quality or productivity performance slip. Children fail to perform assigned chores that help the family prosper. Managers become harsh and mistreat their followers. This breakdown is normal, but it is not acceptable.

Unintentional carelessness or a lack of understanding of the performance goals causes some poor performance. The performance breakdown of others is caused by intentional disregard for the established standards of the organization. Let me be very clear about this. There are some people who get through life by using other people to their own advantage. They become part of an organization just to take from it. These parasites will lie, cheat, steal, and generally disrupt the order of things until they are corrected. Poor performance, whether intentional or unintentional, eventually will destroy any organization. So how can this type of organizational anarchy be prevented, or at least managed? While the answer is not easy, it is relatively simple. Organizational leaders must stay involved enough with their people to accurately evaluate their performances and communicate with them about their strengths and weaknesses. Intentional rebellion or sabotage of the mission cannot be tolerated. Unintentional poor performance may be tolerated for a short time, but it must be corrected.

Information Exchange Systems. Information is power in today's world. People want to be empowered with relevant information so that they can make informed decisions about issues that affect their professional and personal lives. Leaders also have learned that they can depend on their followers to identify problems, find solutions, and even provide encouragement as they press toward the mission. For this reason, it is crucial that an organization have systems in place to communicate significant changes, events, challenges, and successes—both vertically and horizontally. These systems may include bulletin boards, computer mail programs, newsletters, and formal and informal meetings. Most problems in this world to some degree include ineffective communication. Therefore, most problems can be improved with effective communication. We must make sure that people throughout the organization communicate effectively. Information is power, so we need to use it wisely.

Personal Interaction. There is no substitute for positive personal interaction to solidify relationships. This is where the power of agreement is maximized: leaders with leaders, leaders with followers, and followers with followers. Whenever two or more people gather to communicate, some miraculous events can occur. I strongly recommend that leaders of large organizations maintain personal interaction with followers at least two levels below them. I realize that this requires a significant commitment of time, but it is well worth the effort for three reasons. First, it is highly motivating for people to speak face-to-face with those in authority above them. Second, the leader identifies people who as peak performers have promotion potential. Third, though sad but true, some people in positions of leadership abuse the authority with which they are entrusted. In many organizations, these charlatans are able to play this charade for years without getting caught. However, it is amazing how quickly these games stop when each leader communicates directly with people two levels below them.

The ABCs. People are the most valuable resource in virtually every organization in the world. Therefore, it is important to be aware of the condition of each person's *ABCs*—attitudes, behaviors, and communications. Like core values and operating principles, the ABCs must be closely monitored because people change rapidly. Our lives are filled with victories and defeats, births and deaths, celebrations and sorrows. Any of these conditions can occur in a heartbeat, thereby changing what people think, do, and say. These highs and lows of life affect our moods, internal chemistry, life goals, and performance on the job.

Leaders who know their people *personally* can rejoice with them during victories and comfort them in sorrows. This kind of concern and awareness is rewarding for leaders in two ways. First, from an operational perspective, they will have more productive followers who are able to perform at their highest levels. The second reward is more personal. Deep satisfaction comes from successfully leading others into both corporate and personal success. Awareness of the *ABCs* comes when leaders spend time with their most valuable resources: their people.

A CHANGE FOR THE BETTER

At this point, several things should be very clear about change. Change is constant. Change can be unsettling to some people. Change can be negative or positive, depending on how we react to it. Change can be anticipated and managed in ways that create new opportunities, new jobs, new successes, new alliances, and new ways of thinking. What is required to make change something good is a positive outlook and deep commitment to manage the changes that occur in our lives.

I am convinced that we are created with an incredible ability to grow, learn, adjust, and overcome virtually any change that comes our way. Propelled by our visions and guarded by our core values, we can continue to move forward, without fear. Change does not mean that things are getting worse: just that we have new opportunities for growth. We must remember that it takes longer to build something than to tear it apart. A wise craftsman keeps the final product in mind and fights the temptation to rush his work.

The famous sculptor Michelangelo was once asked how he created such beautiful works. He replied that the beauty was always hidden in the block of stone—he simply removed the parts that hid the beauty. I am convinced that we all have a similar opportunity when confronted with change. We can search deep within it to discover the true beauty, and then work diligently to remove whatever prevents others from seeing it as well.

QUESTIONS AND REFLECTIONS

Business • Government • Ministry • Family • Personal

1. Is your organization, in whole or in part, ready for a new way of life? Why?

2. What are the greatest hindrances to your organization's change efforts?

3. What are the greatest strengths that will promote and sustain your organization's change efforts?

4. Are you personally ready for a new way of life?

5. What will result from this new way of life organizationally? Personally?

CHAPTER 18

LESSONS FROM A LEMONADE STAND

The Alaskan wilderness. One of the greatest adventures of my life happened there as I spent seven days catching trophy steelhead trout, sockeye salmon, and full-finned grayling. My guide and I shared the crystal clear rivers with moose, caribou, and giant brown bears that seemed to appear magically when we least expected them. I took this trip in the early 1990s because I needed a change. Life had become too predictable, too structured. After a week of flying through mountain passes in tiny floatplanes and face-to-face encounters with twelve-hundred-pound bears, I was ready to return to my world. As with all journeys that we take, I came back with a new perspective on life. The people, climate, beauty, and challenge of Alaska will do that to you.

I was impressed with how my guide, who had moved his family to Alaska from Chicago, had adjusted to the dramatic change of lifestyle. His discontent with the status quo caused him to follow his dream. Immediately, his life was filled with challenge and change. To build his rustic lodge, he had to have building materials flown in from Anchorage, which was many miles away. There were no stores in the wilderness, so his family, which included his wife Belle and two daughters under the age of six, lived off the land much of the year. It was a delight for me to watch his children enjoying moose burgers much the same as my own children devour the latest fast-food offering from McDonalds. On their lodge wall was the skin of an enormous black bear that had menaced the girls while their father was away. As the story is told, Belle simply walked out the door and dispatched the bear with one shot from her rifle.

Photos of crashed planes and the grizzled guides who lived to tell about them spoke volumes about the risks that accompanied their new way of life. This family had learned to adjust to change and effectively manage it on a daily basis. They lived their lives to the fullest, facing incredible challenges with vision, courage, determination, and patience. Everyone in the family worked together. They were in agreement about their "organization" and its future.

While there, I learned a great deal about managing change. Early each morning, with coffee mug in hand, I would fish from the shore in front of my cabin, usually catching some small trout or salmon. But soon it was time to climb into the pontoon plane that would fly us to remote parts of the wilderness where the fishing was exceptional. The lesson? To catch something special, I had to leave the relative comfort of camp and try something new. The daily floatplane ride itself was an experience—something between exhilaration and terror, depending on the amount of crosswind. Unlike standard aircraft, these little planes have torpedo-shaped aluminum floats instead of wheels. This allows the pilot to take off and land on lakes and rivers. The takeoff is a bit tricky though. The pilot faces the plane into the wind and begins to accelerate across the water. On each takeoff, there is a virtual war of forces as the lifting plane's wings fight to overcome the powerful suction of the water's surface on the pontoons. The pilot has to rock the plane violently from side to side to break free from the water's restraint. Often, this creates bedlam inside the tiny plane as fishing gear and fishermen crash together, until the plane finally is thrust into the sky.

Near the end of my week there, I noticed something amazing. It seemed that the most difficult condition for takeoff was when the surface of the water was *calm*. This condition maximized the suction on the pontoons. It was easier to lift off when the wind whipped the surface of the water into a froth. Another lesson from Alaska: There are times when we want our business, ministry, government, or family to fly to new heights, but we are restrained by the status quo. We often get comfortable with conditions around us, even when those conditions are restrictive and limiting. We, too, must break free from whatever holds us down if we are to go to new places and do new things. To see true change accomplished, we must be willing to endure some shaking and rearranging of our lives, schedules, and priorities. The alternative? We can sit on the beach and catch the small fish while others venture out after the real trophies.

Here's one last Alaskan lesson: We must learn patience and persistence as we pursue our new vision. There were times when our little plane labored halfway across the lake before we were able to finally take off. This, too, has great application for our organizational change efforts. Change takes time; change takes hard work. However, change is worth the effort!

From the wide-open wilderness of Alaska to the cramped confines of the inner city, great things are accomplished each day by ordinary people willing to attempt extraordinary things. In early 1997 I had the pleasure to meet a modern-day hero, Henry T. Baines Sr. Baines, along with his wife and children, moved to Baltimore, Maryland, in 1962. His family was strengthened by faith in God, love for one another, and a desire to accomplish great things. Armed only with a high school diploma and very little money, Baines began his career as a grocery clerk. He was promoted to department manager in three months, and was promoted three more times in four years at that location. By 1978 he had opened his own store. In 1981, he created the Stop Shop Save Corporation that became the largest privately owned grocery chain in Baltimore. Baines has a very unique approach to business growth and community involvement. He demonstrates his commitment to the rejuvenation of Baltimore by locating his stores in neighborhoods that other businesses have abandoned. Rather than locating his stores in new suburban strip malls, Baines renovates discarded and deteriorating buildings, then reopens them to serve people in those communities.

Baines recognizes the importance of motivating and encouraging education of the city's youth through his company's Academic Achievement Awards program that he established in 1978. He began by challenging neighborhood children to bring him their report cards and giving them a reward of money for every good grade that each child achieved. His program has grown exponentially with more trophies, certificates, prizes, and trips awarded every year. Baines, an African American, is an honorary board member of many nonprofit organizations—including the Business Advisory Committee, the NAACP, the President's Roundtable, the Salvation Army, the Baltimore Urban League and the Maryland Food Center Authority.

The dozens of commendations that Baines has received include awards and honors from the U.S. Department of Commerce, Governor William Donald Schaefer, Mayor Kurt L. Schmoke, the 1993 Ernst & Young Award, and *Inc.* magazine's Maryland Retail Entrepreneur of the Year Award. His company was rated number one in Baltimore and number twenty-two nationally in *Black Enterprise* magazine's 1966 list of progressive businesses.

What impresses me so much about Baines is that, by the grace of God and lots of hard work, he has changed his corner of the world for the better. He took what seemed like little and made it into a lot. In 1997, his empire was valued at $100 million and still growing. With all these accomplishments to his credit, Baines easily could coast into early retirement and join the country club set. Will Baltimore lose this shining star to the easy life? Hardly. He is constantly making plans to expand his company's positive impact on his employees, customers, and community. One of his favorite quotes is: "We cannot change yesterday, but today we can, and must, begin to change tomorrow!"

THE LEMONADE STAND

I am reminded of a young boy who many years ago sat on his front porch watching people walk by in the sweltering summer heat. They looked hot, tired, and thirsty as they dragged their feet along the sidewalk. As he thought about their needs, the boy wanted to help.

Suddenly, a new vision was born. He would build a lemonade stand. His ice-cold lemonade would refresh the people and lift their spirits. If he made a great product and served it properly, the people would gladly pay enough to cover his expenses, with enough left over to buy the bicycle that he had always wanted. His vision quickly became a mission, and then a plan. He determined what he would need to build his stand. A list of materials was compiled and construction began. He consulted his grandmother to learn how to make the best-tasting lemonade possible.

The boy reasoned that his venture would grow and that he would need some help serving the customers. He enlisted his brother and sister to work with him. Before they started to work, he taught them about the importance of using the finest ingredients when they made the lemonade and how crucial it was to treat the people with respect. He soon opened his stand for business and served his first customers. Within several days, the people who walked down his street seemed different. They looked forward to stopping at the lemonade stand and talking with the boy. The weather had not changed, but their outlooks had. The young boy's vision had made his part of the world a little better. His vision had become a reality.

The lesson from the lemonade stand is simple. We can sit and watch the world go by, or we can find opportunities to make it better. Parents can passively watch their family relationships disintegrate, or they can actively work to maintain unity and love among family members. Pastors can complain silently about the lack of growth of their churches and devise yet more irrelevant programs to entertain the pew-sitters, or they can challenge and inspire members of their congregations to meet their communities' real needs. Managers with vision can move their employees beyond today's acceptable performance into excellence. The president of a nation either can be satisfied with the status quo or develop a new vision where peace, freedom, and individual opportunities are maximized.

The lesson from the lemonade stand is simple. We can sit and watch the world go by, or we can find opportunities to make it better.

I am convinced that people throughout the world are searching for relevance and greater meaning in their lives. Many are unsure of how to find it, or even what *it* really *is*. We all are hungry for a sense of purpose, something that we can pursue passionately that is greater than ourselves. Today, I invite you to look around your world. What needs are not being met?

What is your passion? What burdens your heart? What is *your* vision? Please take time to think about these questions and write your vision so it is clear to you. Next, share your vision with someone who will agree to support you as you prepare to run this new race toward relevance. Finally, get off the porch and pursue it with all of your heart and soul. In the end, I am certain that you will look back and see that you have changed your world for the better.

QUESTIONS AND REFLECTIONS

Business • Government • Ministry • Family • Personal

1. What is your new vision for your organization or your personal life?

2. What is the next step?

3. What are you waiting for?

Molitor International offers a wide variety of services and resources to help you and your organization succeed. For information on our programs, products, and publications, please contact us by any of the following methods.

Molitor International
1550 Collins Lane
Midland, MI 48640
Phn (989) 832-9730
Fax (989) 835-9993
molitoroffice@tm.net
www.powerofagreement.com